Poverty: A Very Short Introduction

VERY SHORT INTRODUCTIONS are for anyone wanting a stimulating and accessible way into a new subject. They are written by experts, and have been translated into more than 45 different languages.

The series began in 1995, and now covers a wide variety of topics in every discipline. The VSI library currently contains over 550 volumes—a Very Short Introduction to everything from Psychology and Philosophy of Science to American History and Relativity—and continues to grow in every subject area.

Very Short Introductions available now:

Available soon:

For more information visit our website

www.oup.com/vsi/

Philip N. Jefferson

POVERTY

A Very Short Introduction

OXFORD
UNIVERSITY PRESS

Great Clarendon Street, Oxford, OX2 6DP,
United Kingdom

Oxford University Press is a department of the University of Oxford.
It furthers the University's objective of excellence in research, scholarship,
and education by publishing worldwide. Oxford is a registered trade mark of
Oxford University Press in the UK and in certain other countries

© Philip N. Jefferson 2018

The moral rights of the author have been asserted

First edition published in 2018

Impression: 1

All rights reserved. No part of this publication may be reproduced, stored in
a retrieval system, or transmitted, in any form or by any means, without the
prior permission in writing of Oxford University Press, or as expressly permitted
by law, by licence or under terms agreed with the appropriate reprographics
rights organization. Enquiries concerning reproduction outside the scope of the
above should be sent to the Rights Department, Oxford University Press, at the
address above

You must not circulate this work in any other form
and you must impose this same condition on any acquirer

Published in the United States of America by Oxford University Press
198 Madison Avenue, New York, NY 10016, United States of America

British Library Cataloguing in Publication Data
Data available

Library of Congress Control Number: 2018933086

ISBN 978-0-19-871647-1

Printed in Great Britain by
Ashford Colour Press Ltd, Gosport, Hampshire

Links to third party websites are provided by Oxford in good faith and
for information only. Oxford disclaims any responsibility for the materials
contained in any third party website referenced in this work.

For Nathan and Miles

Contents

Acknowledgements

I thank Maureen Callahan, Stephen O'Connell, and Clint Bartlett for helpful discussions. Andrea Keegan and Jenny Nugée of Oxford University Press and anonymous referees provided constructive feedback for which I am grateful. I extend a special thanks to Alison Howson whose editorial judgement and skill improved this book significantly. Finally, I thank students in my course on poverty and inequality. Their questions and comments catalyse clarity of thought and expression. I am solely responsible for any errors and omissions that remain.

Philip N. Jefferson

Swarthmore, Pennsylvania
USA
March 2018

List of illustrations

Development Centre, December 2014 <https://www.oecd.org/dev/ development-gender/Unpaid: care_work.pdf.

OECD Secretariat estimates based on national time-use surveys. Data are for the latest year available as of 2014. <http:// www.oecd.org/gender/data/ time-spent-in-unpaid-paid-and-total-work-by-sex.htm Accessed 26 July 2017>.

Poverty

List of abbreviations

AROPE	at risk of poverty or social exclusion
CAP	Community Action Program
DAC	Development Assistance Committee
EITC	Earned Income Tax Credit
FDR	Franklin Delano Roosevelt
FHA	Federal Housing Administration
GDP	gross domestic product
HDI	Human Development Index
IMF	International Monetary Fund
MDGs	Millennium Development Goals
NSDC	National Skill Development Corporation
ODA	official development assistance
OECD	Organization for Economic Co-operation and Development
OEO	Office of Economic Opportunity
PISA	Program for International Student Assessment
PPP	purchasing power parity
RCT	randomized control trial
RPP&E	Research, Programming, Planning, and Evaluation
SDGs	Sustainable Development Goals
UC	Universal Credit

Chapter 1
Introduction

Pervasiveness and trends

Poverty is a global issue. Travel to almost any country today and you will see people with a standard of living that is significantly lower than that of others. That fact is distressing and it has real consequences for adults and children living in poverty. Nevertheless, the absolute number of people living in poverty represents a marked improvement over that in 1990, especially in the poorest countries in the world. Therefore, there is reason to hope that further poverty reduction can occur.

Tables 1 and 2 show the poverty rate and the number of people living in poverty in the developing world. In 2013, approximately 11 per cent of people, or 766 million people, in the world lived on less than $1.90 per day. In 1990, these numbers stood at 35 per cent, or 1.8 billion people. In less than twenty-five years, more than a billion people graduated out of extreme poverty. By looking at the data across regions, we can see where we are winning the fight against poverty and where we are not. In terms of percentages and absolute numbers, the East Asia and Pacific region, led by China and Indonesia, experienced the greatest reduction in poverty. South Asia, which includes India, was also impressive in this regard. In contrast, over the same time frame, extreme poverty in sub-Saharan Africa fell in percentage

Table 1 Percentage of population in extreme poverty

Region	1990	2002	2010	2013
World	34.8	25.3	15.6	10.7
East Asia and Pacific	60.2	29.0	11.1	3.5
Europe and Central Asia	1.9	6.3	2.9	2.2
Latin America and the Caribbean	15.8	13.0	6.5	5.4
Middle East and North Africa	6.0	—	—	—
South Asia	44.6	38.5	24.6	15.1
Sub-Saharan Africa	54.3	55.6	45.7	41.0

N.B. $1.90 per day poverty line; dashes indicate insufficient data to determine. To account for differences in cost of living across regions, prices are set at 2011 purchasing power parity.

Source: PovcalNet, World Bank.

Table 2 Number of people in extreme poverty

Region	1990	2002	2010	2013
World	1,840.5	1,588.1	1,076.9	766.0
East Asia and Pacific	965.9	535.1	218.2	71.0
Europe and Central Asia	8.9	29.3	13.7	10.3
Latin America and the Caribbean	71.2	70.6	38.8	33.6
Middle East and North Africa	13.7	—	—	—
South Asia	505.0	552.4	400.3	256.2
Sub-Saharan Africa	276.1	391.3	399.1	388.7

N.B. Number (in millions). $1.90 per day poverty line; dashes indicate insufficient data to determine. To account for differences in cost of living across regions, prices are set at 2011 purchasing power parity.

Source: PovcalNet, World Bank.

terms but rose in absolute number, so much so that in 2013, about half of the people living in poverty worldwide were concentrated in this region. In Chapter 7, we will consider economic factors and policies that explain why countries in East Asia and Pacific excelled in poverty reduction, while sub-Saharan Africa countries did not.

Poverty, however, is not restricted to the developing world. Developed countries have their own brand of poverty. We consider how that brand differs qualitatively from that in the developing world in Chapter 4. Suffice it to say that people experience poverty in the developed world relative to those who are not poor that is akin, if not in kind, to those living in poverty in the developing world. Therefore, concern for expanding opportunities that might improve their well-being is justified. The past twenty-five years have yielded mixed results in poverty reduction in the developed world, as the United Kingdom and the United States exemplify.

Table 3 shows that while the poverty rate in the United Kingdom has fallen by 6 per cent, the number of people living in poverty has only dropped by two million in actual number. As in much of Western Europe, the concept of poverty reported here is a relative one. The poverty line is 60 per cent of median household income of the total population. In the United States, the poverty rate has been static over the past quarter century as shown in Table 4. The number of people in poverty, however, has drifted upward in line with population growth. The US government bases its official poverty rate on a concept of poverty that is absolute, meaning that the poverty line reflects a fixed level of basic needs. In Chapter 3, we spell out the differences between absolute and relative concepts of poverty. The important point to take away from Table 3 and Table 4 is that in the UK and the US, we see nothing like the progress against poverty that we have seen in the developing world.

The results for the UK and the US are common to those in other developed nations: an absence of dramatic declines in poverty

Table 3 Poverty in the United Kingdom

	1990	2002	2010	2013	2015
Rate	22.2	18.4	16.9	15.4	15.9
Number (millions)	12.1	10.4	10.4	9.7	10.1

N.B. The poverty rate is the number of people whose income falls below the poverty line divided by the population. The poverty line is 60 per cent of median household income of the total population. Income measure is before deduction of housing costs. Based on data from the Institute for Fiscal Studies, with kind permission.

Table 4 Poverty in the United States

	1990	2002	2010	2013	2015
Rate	13.5	12.1	15.1	14.8	13.5
Number (millions)	33.6	34.6	46.3	46.2	43.1

N.B. The poverty rate is the number of people whose income falls below the poverty line divided by the population. The poverty line reflects a fixed level of basic needs.

Source: United States Bureau of the Census.

over the past quarter century. Why? One argument is that there was less poverty in rich countries to begin with and hence there is less room for reducing the poverty rate further. A counter-argument to this is, why not use our considerable wealth to eliminate the poverty that remains? Another argument is that poor people in rich countries are not actually poor. They have amenities of which truly poor people, such as those in developing countries, could only dream. Hence, society need not do any more to help lift people out of poverty. Here, a counter-argument is that we made a false comparison. At its core, poverty is contextual. What matters is an individual's well-being relative to the community in which she exists.

Contextual aspects

We need look no further than a kitchen to discern that poverty is contextual. In India, a family living in poverty is likely to use a

1. Wood-burning stove in India.

traditional wood-burning stove as in Figure 1. It is functional but it also exposes the family to a number of risks including repeated exposure to carbon and particulate emissions that may eventually undermine the family's health. If this stove compromises the health of adult family members, then it will also reduce their earnings capacity and increase the likelihood that the family remains in poverty. If it compromises the health of children family members, then they will attend school less frequently. Therefore, they will learn less over time and have limited employment opportunities when they get older. In this way, intergenerational transmission of poverty may occur, as discussed in Chapter 6.

In the US, 97 per cent of people living in poverty have a cooking stove. Figure 2 shows a basic version of one. This modest stove runs on electricity. It is easy to operate, highly functional, and it does not pollute the home. Yet, from the perspective of a wealthy American family, this basic stove might be considered wholly inadequate because it does not have certain amenities such as an embedded clock and timer, a digital interface, a self-cleaning function, a convection fan, automatic shut-off, temperature sensor

2. Basic electric stove.

baking, or an interior light. To top that list off, it does not even have a window in the oven door! Therefore, while an Indian family living in poverty might consider a basic electric stove a luxury, an American family living in poverty would consider it an entry-level appliance of which there are vastly superior versions that are far beyond the family's reach.

Beyond the observation that poverty is contextual, our kitchen stove example hints at the material inequality that exists both within and across nations. An American living in poverty may seem wealthy to an Indian living in poverty because the former has an electric stove. That same American may seem poor to another American living at median income in the United States because the former has to manage with a stove that is not self-cleaning. In Chapter 6, we discuss inequality. We also consider how its severity can impede graduation out of poverty. Before getting to that issue, however, we will see in Chapter 4 that contrasts between people living in poverty in different parts of the world extend beyond their kitchens to things like their life expectancy and their typical family structure. Nevertheless, what is perhaps more striking are similarities between these same people. In their context, insufficient access to quality schooling, healthcare, and employment constrains them. These factors, however, are not the only ones that drive narratives about why people are poor.

Causes

No one wants to live in poverty. Yet, many people do live in poverty. Why is that? Over time, observers have proposed many causes of poverty, including dysfunctional institutions, discrimination, low social capital, social exclusion, low human capital, social stratification, residential segregation, the business cycle, unemployment, low wages, poor health, culture, shifting norms about family structure, technological advance and industrialization, globalization and the expansion of international trade, holes in the social safety net, and anti-poverty policy itself.

Institutions are the rules we live by. Dysfunctional institutions impede innovation and broad participation in economic and political life. Rules that create significant imbalances in economic and political power can suppress returns that individuals and groups receive from their work and can exclude them from processes that permit them to voice their political will. Such rules undermine incentives to engage in productive activities. For example, a farmer whose claim to land ownership is insecure due to a government's weak enforcement of property rights is less likely to invest in maintenance or enrichment of her land. Therefore, the farm will be less productive than it otherwise could have been. If the problem is severe, the farmer may decide to stop farming altogether and to shift to another activity to which she is less well suited. As a result, weak property rights enforcement exposes the one-time farmer to a higher risk of impoverishment.

Discrimination excludes people from resources and opportunity. Underlying it is the notion that something valuable like high-quality jobs, housing, education, or healthcare is scarce. The perception of scarcity can induce utilization of arbitrary characteristics such as race, gender, language, ethnicity, sexual orientation, or religious belief as a basis for restricting access to basic goods and services that sustain well-being. People who discriminate put members of the discriminated-against group at a disadvantage, particularly if the characteristic on which discrimination is based is readily observable. For example, if you live in a society where there is discrimination based on race and you are a member of a disfavoured racial group or caste, then your chances of restricted access to quality housing, healthcare, and a good job is higher, your level of education notwithstanding.

Who among us does not know someone who got a job or found a place to live or gained membership into a particular club as a result of knowing someone in a position to either provide a key introduction or to close the deal himself or herself? Perhaps we, ourselves, are the ones who have benefited from such an occurrence. Personal networks that can deliver such meaningful economic and social outcomes are a part of one's *social capital*. We build these networks over time and intertwine them with networks of others with whom we have professional and social contact. The position of our family members, close friends, and even acquaintances in the existing social hierarchy of society determines the potency of our social capital. The better the position of these individuals, the more likely it is that our individual talents will catapult us within that same social hierarchy. What if, for reasons beyond your control, you do not know someone who knows someone? Then, you do not have much social capital. Then, it is less likely that you will receive the tip that, for example, a job for which you have trained is about to become available at a business across town because of a pending transfer of a current employee. Alternatively, it is less likely that someone will recommend you to assume the lease of that apartment in that neighbourhood surrounded by a bevy of start-up firms looking for new employees. Further, it is less likely that someone will connect you to the right person who can get your child into the right pre-school; you know the one, whose graduates gain access to the best primary schools.

There are people who work regularly, sometimes holding down multiple jobs, yet live in poverty because their wages are low. According to economic orthodoxy, their low earnings are likely to reflect the fact that they are relatively unskilled and/or not well educated. That is, they have low *human capital*. The amount of human capital you possess is a function of past schooling, training, and experience. It is a determinant of how productive you are likely to be in the workplace. For example, if, because of your education and training, you are able to read, calculate, and write both quickly and effectively, then it is more likely that you will be highly valued by an employer. A manifestation of your value will be greater compensation relative to someone with less education. We can only go so far, however, with the viewpoint that productivity is the sole determinant of wages, earnings, or compensation. We know that other factors such as custom and bargaining power also matter. For example, just a few decades ago, it would have been unseemly for the chief executive officer of a firm to make more than thirty times the salary of the average staff employee. That ethos has eroded in many countries worldwide. Labour unions, once a bulwark against the power of management to set wages unilaterally, have seen a decline in membership and effectiveness to the detriment of workers at the lower end of the pay distribution.

Residential segregation circumscribes educational, employment, and healthcare opportunities whenever there are geographical restrictions on enrolment, insufficient or inequitable public funding, or transportation costs. Typically, there are catchment areas for schools and considerable heterogeneity in the quality of schools because of how societies fund them. For example, if local property taxes fund schools, then the quality of educational facilities, the curriculum, and, most importantly, the teachers will vary according to the wealth of the community. With this funding structure, low-wealth communities are likely to have low-performing schools. More generally, it is more likely that poverty traps people allocated to a residential area with under-resourced schools and few employment options. We say 'allocated' because historically where low-income people can live has often been a manifestation of public policy. The researcher Richard Rothstein documents government allocative policies in the United States. For example, the Federal Housing Administration (FHA) practised 'redlining' from the mid-1930s to the late 1960s. It refused to insure the mortgages of African Americans who wished to purchase homes in white neighbourhoods regardless of their creditworthiness. This practice limited where African Americans could live. The FHA even went further by refusing to insure the mortgages of creditworthy whites who wished to purchase homes in or even near African American neighbourhoods. Not surprisingly, the net effect of redlining was neighbourhoods segregated by race. Such policies are one source of the high level of racial segregation that we see across the United States today. Another historical example is the government policy of apartheid in South Africa from 1948 to 1994 that sought to minimize interactions between whites and people of colour, especially blacks. One component of this policy was severe restrictions on land ownership by blacks that relegated them to substandard housing and all of its concomitant perils.

Cultural explanations of poverty span the gamut. One viewpoint is that people live in poverty because they harbour deviant morals, values, and behaviour. The idea underlying this viewpoint is that somehow people living in poverty are fundamentally different from other people in society. They are lazy and looking for a handout. They do not have enough resilience or determination. They do not have grit. They are responsible for their plight. If only they would change their attitudes and behaviours, their lives would be different. An alternative viewpoint is that the values of people living in poverty are no different from the rest of society. In response to social and economic conditions such as racism and systemic exclusion, people living in poverty develop patterns of behaviour that enable them to cope and to survive. For example, the US has high incarceration rates relative to other industrialized nations. Over two-thirds of incarcerated men are between the ages of 25 and 50, a prime age range for marriage. Consequentially, single motherhood may be a response to a decline in the availability of marriageable men.

More broadly, shifting norms about *family structure* mean that women and men have more options for arranging their social affairs. When we add children to the equation, women, in particular, are less constrained by custom to do what may not be in their best interest. In societies where women are paid less than men for comparable work and where there is weak public support for income maintenance during labour market absences due to childbearing, particular family structures, such as households headed by single women, are at higher risk of experiencing episodes of poverty.

Many societies are hierarchical with the structure of a multidimensional lattice. This structure is the result of interstitial relations along the lines of gender, class, educational attainment, race, and ethnicity. Movement across the nodes of intersection can be challenging because there are barriers that preserve the existing *stratification*. Stakeholders want to preserve the status quo. In a stratified society, some group or groups of people matriculate at the bottom rungs simply because they have the 'wrong' attributes either singly or in combination. History provides us with examples of stratified societies based on caste, race, and religion. This is not to say that stratification is anachronistic. We see it in modern societies as the preservation of privilege through restricted access for some people to the best schools, healthcare, and housing. People born into poverty in such societies face a labyrinth of obstacles to social mobility.

Technological advance and *industrialization* have undoubtedly enriched us on average over the long run, but they have also been a source of displacement of workers with obsolete skills, farm workers, and artisans. For example, the Industrial Revolution in England saw the release of many skilled textile workers in the wake of the introduction of mechanized production methods. More recently, widespread use of computers and robotics induced the release of traditional assembly-line workers in manufacturing. Displaced workers with obsolete skills may integrate into the new economy slowly. The transition can be both immiserating and psychologically traumatic.

Globalization, the enhanced freedom of movement of people, goods, and capital, and the expansion of *international trade*, is a positive phenomenon on balance. Its benefits, however, are widely diffused. These benefits can seem insignificant compared to the losses experienced by those harmed by increased competition in trade. The benefits of globalization can be lower prices for goods and increased variety, which most consumers enjoy. Its costs can take the form of redundant production plants and equipment and localized job losses, especially when local labour is immobile. For example, the economist David Autor and his collaborators show that communities in the United States with industries that compete with cheap imports from China have experienced significant employment loss, wage declines, and an increase in transfer payments from government.

Policymakers design *anti-poverty policies* to assist people living in poverty and to promote graduation from poverty. Policies that provide assistance seek to support the poor by providing cash, services, or goods in amounts to prevent people from falling below a minimal standard of basic needs. For example, unconditional monthly cash payments to a household would allow the head of household to buy food so that the caloric intake of household members does not fall below those needed for human growth and development. Households could use these same cash payments for clothing and shelter. Policies that promote graduation from poverty seek to pave the way for people to achieve a sustainable level of income that is above a given poverty threshold. For example, a programme that provides job training, employment counselling, and employment referrals to individuals living in poverty could enable them to gain lasting employment and an enduring attachment to the labour force. A good job has the potential for professional growth, some autonomy, and benefits (a workplace pension and a health plan).

It is possible, however, that all of these policies, while well intentioned, are misguided. Critics argue that they distort behaviour and that people respond better to incentives. If anti-poverty policy is too generous, then people are less inclined to work, save, and invest in themselves. They become reliant on government for support: they sit back and let the rest of society care for them. In the absence of these policies, would-be beneficiaries have a strong incentive to become self-sufficient, industrious, and entrepreneurial. Anti-poverty policy, by logical extension, causes poverty because it incentivizes dependency on social provision of benefits. Why work when the government rewards not working? To go further, critics point out that anti-poverty policy penalizes financially those who want to work more by incorporating very high marginal income tax rates. Consider a conditional cash transfer programme based on labour supply behaviour. When participants first start to work, cash transfers paid to them supplement their earnings. This creates a strong incentive to work. Once earnings reach a certain level, however, the government reduces the amount of the transfer gradually. Then, when earnings reach an even higher level, the transfer is withdrawn entirely. During this so-called phase-out range, the government penalizes each dollar earned by the amount of the reduction in the transfer received. In the phase-out range of conditional cash transfer programmes based on labour supply, the implicit marginal tax rate on earned income can be quite high. This high marginal tax rate could create a disincentive to work more. We discuss examples of this kind of programme in Chapter 3 and Chapter 5.

An opposing viewpoint is that holes in the social safety net cause persistent poverty. Most Western societies have a system of programmes designed to help those that it deems worthy of support (the so-called deserving poor). Historical examples include widows, orphans, and the elderly. Then, there are those that society deems undeserving of public support. Historically, these are prime-aged adults who do not appear to be contributing to society by working and paying their share of taxes. When job loss occurs because of the vicissitudes of life such as ill health (mental or physical) or acts of nature, then individuals and families with limited financial reserves are vulnerable regardless of their stage of life. A robust social safety net can be all that stands between sudden misfortune and destitution.

For some people, *poor health* is a chronic condition. Bad health, permanent mental or physical illness, or disability restricts them from carrying out normal activities of life such as dressing and bathing, much less working on a regular basis. Chronic physical or mental illness is debilitating. Individuals living with chronic illness are at greater risk of living in poverty, especially if they do not have the support of family and friends. Generally, they are unable to work. Leaves of absence to accommodate pain and recovery disrupt workflows and reduce an employee's value to the firm. Absenteeism increases the likelihood of termination of employment.

The economic climate also plays a role in the availability of good and reliable employment. *Economic recessions* are broad-based declines in economic activity. Retail sales and the production of goods and services fall during recessions. In response to weak demand for goods and services, firms slow down production and reduce hours or staff numbers. *Unemployment* rises during recessions and people lose their jobs. These job losses cause income to fall. Housing construction is an example of a cyclically sensitive industry that employs a large number of people of various skill levels. When the macroeconomy is doing well, unskilled workers are able to find steady employment in this sector. When there is a slump, unskilled labourers are among the first that firms lay off in the housing sector. For low-income households, an episode of unemployment experienced by one or more family members can mean living in poverty. This poverty is due to macroeconomic conditions. Its antidote is a revival in aggregate demand that leads to economic expansion. When the economy expands, firms are more willing to hire or rehire employees. For many families temporary poverty ends with macroeconomic recovery.

This list of the causes of poverty is not exhaustive. It highlights, however, some of the complex issues and situations that push people into poverty and hold them there. Each individual or family has its own story. Some of these causes have received more factual support than others have. These causes embed themselves in social, political, economic, educational, and technological processes that affect all of us from the time we are born until we die. Our degree of vulnerability is all that differentiates us. How vulnerable you are or are not to adverse changes in your life is a function of the circumstances of your birth, including where your family lived, which schools you attended, whether it was peacetime or wartime, whether you had access to clean water, whether you are male or female. The list goes on and on.

Why poverty matters

As Table 3 shows, poverty in the United Kingdom rose by 0.5 percentage points between 2013 and 2015 as 400,000 more people fell into poverty. In June of 2016, to the surprise of many in the UK and much of the world, the majority of citizens voted to leave the European Union, so-called Brexit. While there is no simple reason for this outcome, there is little doubt that the perception of widespread economic insecurity in the UK contributed to what many consider a political upheaval, an intentional severing of ties with rest of Europe that were forty-three years in the making. It is certainly fair to ask, would the outcome of the vote have been different if citizens of the UK felt their economic status was less precarious?

Also in 2016, in the province of Kasserine, Tunisia, public protests over the high level of unemployment broke out after a young man, Ridha Yahyaoui, committed suicide because the government left his name off a list of candidates for a government job. The protesters' demands were for jobs and a solution to the poverty gripping the province. The protest in Kasserine triggered protests in other cities in Tunisia, including the capital, Tunis. The government's initial response was a nationwide curfew from sunset to sunrise. The aggregate unemployment rate in Tunisia had risen over the previous two years and in 2016 hovered around 15.5 per cent. This aggregate unemployment rate, however, masked the unemployment rate among young people with university degrees. That rate was closer to 30 per cent in 2016. The protesters in the streets were predominately young people who were desperate for jobs but could not find work. If these circumstances sound familiar, it is because they are; for it was in Tunisia in 2011 that mass demonstrations that we know now as the 'Arab Spring' began after the self-immolation of Mohamed Bouazizi in December 2010. In Tunisia, these demonstrations led to the toppling of the government of then-president Zine El Abidine Ben Ali.

These examples from the developed and the developing world highlight why poverty matters. Widespread economic insecurity and the poverty it induces negatively affect the lifetime prospects of individuals and families. It can be a source of social unrest and political upheaval. In the face of a fraying social fabric, societies have to decide how to respond. Those responses often depend upon attitudes (philosophical, religious, political, social, or economic) towards people living in poverty.

Can a just society include many people living in poverty? The philosopher John Rawls provides one perspective on this question. His difference principle would allow an inequitable distribution of income as long as any further increment in inequality resulted in an increase in the absolute level of well-being of the poorest in society. It follows that in the design of public policy there would be no restriction on individual earnings or wealth. There would be scope, however, for redistribution of income to the neediest.

We know that attitudes about redistributive policies vary across countries. In the United States, the tendency to label any individual espousing favourable views about redistribution as 'socialist' circumscribes explicit political discourse on redistributive policies. In the European context, there is more space to advocate for redistributive policies. Increasingly, however, the narrative focuses on redistribution extending only to beneficiaries who are citizens. In the developing country context, frequently the government's capacity to collect taxes is so weak that the idea of implementing redistributive policies is beyond the practical scope of society's institutions.

If the government is unwilling or unable to assist people living in poverty, then who can or will? As will be discussed in more detail in Chapter 2, historically, the answer to this question is the church, charities, and private individuals. An individual could have strong views about his or her community and harbour concerns about acts of begging that can arise because of widespread poverty. Led by one's faith, and perhaps consideration of what it teaches about the path to heaven, an individual could contribute to the well-being of those living in poverty by contributing to them directly or by giving to one's church. Then, the church could pool the contributions of many people and aid those living in poverty by providing shelter, food, clothing, and even education. From this perspective, poverty matters because it provides individuals with an opportunity to enhance the well-being of others while practising certain principles of their faith. Although private charity and the church have always played a role in addressing poverty, it is rarely enough to provide relief to all who need it.

Overall, the economy suffers if systematic public policy does not address poverty. Poverty imposes costs on the economy due to lost human capital and poor resource allocation. Poverty accelerates the depreciation of any economy's most valuable resource, its people, by depriving them of quality healthcare and education. It drives people to engage in activities from begging to multiple low-wage jobs that are less than ideal, in the sense that they could spend their time more productively in specialized employment.

Poverty is a stain on the fabric of society. Widespread and persistent poverty can sow the seeds of discontent based on a loss of dignity associated with a feeling of exclusion from society. Feelings of indignity, alienation, and disrespect can fuel crime, large-scale public protests, and even extremist ideologies that lead to terrorism. Generally, removal or diminution of this stain requires public action by government with the consent and cooperation of the governed.

This book is an introduction into the various forms of public and private actions that societies have taken and are currently undertaking in the struggle against poverty. Access to and participation in the conversation about poverty presumes knowledge of a few key definitions and theoretical concepts, a bit of history, familiarity with a some data, and the intuition behind a methodology for determining cause and effect. We cover this terrain in this book. I invite you into the conversation about poverty.

Chapter 2
History

Prehistory

Poverty is an ancient problem. In the pre-modern period, poverty was synonymous with hunger. In nomadic societies, physical disability could put the welfare of individuals and families at risk. The ability to track and hunt a herd of migrating animals would have been essential for survival on the African savannah. In agricultural societies, crop failures due to droughts, floods, or warfare caused famine and poverty. With the emergence of the market economy where using money to trade dominates barter, the kind of poverty that we recognize today arose. This was due to factors both within and across societies that have negative effects on vulnerable people. The distinction between factors acting within and/or across societies provides a lens for interpreting particular historical episodes.

Emergence and response

Before the 16th century, agriculture was the leading sector of many societies. Most of the population worked in the agricultural sector. The manorial system of the Middle Ages in Europe provides one example of how this sector was organized. In this system, peasants, of which there were many, worked land owned by lords. Peasants paid the manor lord either a fixed amount of each harvest or rent for use of the land. Key features of this system were crop rotation, common land, and strip-farming of open land. Crop rotation was the practice of allowing a fraction of farmland to lay fallow for some period. This allowed farm animals to graze the land. Their manure revitalized the soil. Commons were part of the manor land that was free for everyone to use for various activities including gathering firewood and grazing cattle. Strip-farming was the practice of dividing arable land into long rows or strips. The manor lord allocated each peasant-farmer strips in different areas and quality of arable land. In a society based on subsistence farming, this allocation strategy was a form of risk-sharing by peasants working open land. No single family worked crops only on the best or worse part of the land.

There was not much of a response to poverty by ruling elites or governments. People living in poverty relied on their extended family, their local community, and the church for support. The church assisted widows, orphans, and people who were physically disabled; people the church deemed to be deserving of assistance. God had intervened and left them unable to support themselves. It was part of the Christian church's teaching that parishioners extend charity to them. The church did not think that able-bodied adults living in poverty were deserving of assistance.

Advances in farming techniques led to an enclosing of arable common land in England. Eventually, enclosure would contribute to ending the manorial system in Europe. Enclosure was the process of merging leased small landholdings of several peasant-farmers into larger farms owned by one farmer. Under enclosure, land use shifted from arable subsistence farming to uses such as rearing sheep for wool that were more profitable. The enclosure movement preceded the Industrial Revolution in England. Some would argue that enclosure was a catalyst for the Industrial Revolution because of the profits enclosure generated for landowners and traders. A significant side effect of enclosure, however, was the release of a large number of peasant-farmers. Landowners no longer needed their labour. Thus, enclosure represented a structural change that displaced many peasant-farmers from the countryside and drove them into towns for work. Enclosure was also a source of inequality within society. Now, there was a class of labourers, divorced from the land, and too large in number for firms to absorb in nascent industrial towns. These displaced workers and their families were at great risk of living in poverty. Displaced peasant-farmers in England had their parallels in France, Germany, Spain, and Italy. Of course, the hardship faced by displaced peasants in France fuelled the Revolution that would eventually take place there.

In the 16th and 17th centuries, there were societal and government responses to poverty. A significant development in this regard was the English Poor Laws. These laws empowered local parish authorities to impose taxes on residents in order to offer 'poor relief' to people living in poverty. They also made local parishes responsible for destitute people living in their parishes. One reason for this public response was that people living in poverty were numerous, concentrated, and visible. Relief took the form of food, clothing, and small amounts of money for the so-called deserving poor. Its main purpose was to provide an alternative to begging which localities frequently banned. Criminalization of begging meant that people living in poverty were subject to punishment. Their punishment could take the form of public whipping or incarceration in workhouses. Workhouses were institutions designed to correct attitudes towards work by providing opportunities to perform menial tasks, while providing only the bare minimum of nutrition. A goal of workhouses was the redemption of people living in poverty. The authorities thought that their impoverishment was due to their bad habits (laziness or profligacy). English workhouses had their parallels in other Western European countries and North America.

In the 18th century, Adam Smith achieved a systematic understanding of how and why markets work through observation and careful study. Additionally, his identification of linen shirt ownership as a prerequisite for acceptance into proper society underscored the role of social inclusion in well-being. The discipline of economics grew out of his conception of specialization, self-interest, and trade in providing for the greater good. Thomas Robert Malthus, one the other hand, was concerned with the prospect of mass starvation. His view was that population increased exponentially while food production increased only arithmetically. As a result, population would eventually outstrip the available food supply. The inability to provision a subsistence level of food intake is perhaps the most severe form of impoverishment. David Ricardo saw a world divided into sharp social classes: workers, capitalists, and landlords. For Ricardo, the distribution of national income between classes was a concern. Workers received wages, capitalists received profits, and landlords received rents. In Ricardo's view, landlords grew rich over time because the supply of land was fixed. Land commanded more rent as economic activity expanded. Competitive pressures squeezed capitalists' profits. Workers' standard of living would stay low because wage increases induced population increases that in turn dissipated wage increases. Based on the work of Malthus and Ricardo, economics earned the label, the 'dismal' science. Then, there was Karl Marx, who believed that Ricardo's working class would eventually rise up in revolt against their impoverished status. They would organize themselves and undo the capitalist system.

In the causes of poverty overviewed in Chapter 1, we hear echoes of Smith, Malthus, Ricardo, and Marx. Smith whispers to us when we speak of social exclusion. Malthus whispers to us when we speak of family structure. Ricardo whispers to us when we speak of income inequality. Marx whispers to us when we speak of redistribution.

Colonialism

By the early 19th century, there was a significant degree of inequality across countries. The economic historian Angus Maddison documents that per capita income in Western Europe was, on average, twice that of the rest of the world. The gap between the West and the rest was due in part to Europe's early industrialization, acquisition of colonies, and slavery. Primary products produced by colonies fed into the emerging industrial and luxury consumer goods sector in Western Europe. As profits accumulated and colonists reinvested them in Western Europe, the gap in economic well-being between it and the rest of the world grew.

It is difficult to say when Western colonialism began in earnest. Was it with Spain in the Canary Islands in 1402? Was it with Queen Elizabeth I's grant of a royal charter to the English East India Company in 1600? The precise date is less important than the enrichment that accrued to Western European countries because of extractive institutions and policies.

An example is the plantation system for sugar and cotton production. Driven by the desire to maximize profit, it required that plantation owners pay labour little or nothing beyond what labourers needed to maintain the strength to work. Supported by the Atlantic slave trade, which began in the 16th century, the plantation system proliferated in the Americas and the Caribbean. Alexander Hamilton, one of America's founding fathers, grew up in the Caribbean (on Nevis and St Croix) in the 1750s and 1760s. Caribbean sugar plantations were a source of enormous wealth for England and Europe. Hamilton's biographer, Ron Chernow, characterizes the Caribbean plantation system of Hamilton's youth as one of 'inimitable savagery, making the tobacco and cotton plantations of the American south seem almost genteel by comparison. The mortality rate of slaves hacking away at sugarcane under a pitiless tropical sun was simply staggering: three out of five died within five years of arrival.'

Here was a source of poverty that has lasted down the centuries. It paid no respect to protective structures such as family or pre-existing social arrangements. It represented the commodification of human beings to such an extent that it was common to view enslaved people as less than fully human. Such sentiment was included in the American Constitution of 1787. The enslaved black population of each state counted for only three-fifths of their total number when calculating a state's population used for assigning congressional representation. Perniciously, enslavement of people from sub-Saharan Africa in the European colonies imbued the institution of slavery with a racial overlay and the vulgar implication that dark-skinned people were subhuman. A legacy of this vulgarity is the racial discrimination that exists in the Americas, including the United States, and the Caribbean today. In Chapter 1, we saw how public policies that mandated race-based residential segregation supported discrimination against blacks in the US that lasted into the late 1960s. It is not surprising that there is a high degree of residential segregation by race in the US currently.

Another example of the legacy of colonial discrimination comes to us from South Africa. The Dutch colonized South Africa originally. The British took over, beginning in the 17th century. The discovery of diamonds in the 19th century raised the value of land there and stimulated settlers' desire to control the land and the indigenous population. These desires evolved into the system of apartheid discussed in Chapter 1. South Africa began to dismantle that system in the 1990s. Yet, we see in the photography of Johnny Miller an example of current living conditions based on race. On the left of Figure 3, we see the area of Masiphumelele where blacks live in little more than shacks. On the right, we see a luxurious lakefront community where whites live. In-between is a buffer zone that separates the two communities. This snapshot,

3. Housing segregation in South Africa.

taken in 2016, is not atypical of housing arrangements in South Africa. The juxtaposition of current housing conditions provide stark evidence of the persistent impact of colonization and the policies that followed from it.

Colonizers justified their actions by referring to the so-called backwardness of indigenous people. Often indigenous societies exhibited institutions and ways of being that contrasted with those recognizable to the Europeans who first met them. We read in Christopher Columbus' letter (February 1493) to Luis de St Angel about his first contact with indigenous people in the West Indies that 'In all these islands the men seem to be satisfied with one wife, except they allow as many as twenty to their chief or king. The women appear to me to work harder than the men, and so far as I can hear they have nothing of their own, for I think I perceived that what one had others shared, especially food.' And 'The only arms they have are sticks of cane, cut when in seed with a sharpened stick at the end, and they are afraid to use these.' And 'they are so unsuspicious and so generous with what they possess, that no one who had not seen it would believe it. They never refuse anything that is asked for. They even offer it themselves, and show so much love that they would give their very hearts.'

26

From this, Columbus concludes, 'Therefore I hope that their Highnesses will decide upon the conversion of these people to our holy faith, to which they seem much inclined.'

Europeans settlers perceived themselves as advanced technologically and culturally. Sanctioned by the church, they believed that they had a moral obligation to bring indigenous populations to what they saw as the frontier of religious, social, and economic organization. If indigenous societies resisted settlers' overtures to adopt European religious, social, and economic practices, then conquest was justified because Europeans viewed the freedom to trade as a fundamental right. Thus, Europeans settlers rationalized conquest on a grand scale. The church also sanctioned it. If fulfilment of their obligation meant enslavement, then that was justified at least until the indigenous societies began to exhibit traits of European society. A concise statement of this perspective is contained in the *Requirement* of the Council of Castile (Spain, 1510). After proclaiming the dominion of the Pope over all men and the requirement that indigenous people convert to Christianity, it concludes that in response to any resistance at all,

> we shall powerfully enter into your country, and shall make war against you in all ways and manners that we can, and shall subject you to the yoke and obedience of the Church and of their Highnesses; we shall take you and your wives and your children, and shall make slaves of them, and as such shall sell and dispose of them as their Highnesses may command; and we shall take away your goods, and shall do you all the mischief and damage that we can, as to vassals who do not obey, and refuse to receive their lord, and resist and contradict him; and we protest that the deaths and losses which shall accrue from this are your fault, and not that of their Highnesses, or ours, nor of these cavaliers who come with us.

This requirement did not bode well for the indigenous people of Mexico (Aztecs) when the Spanish arrived there in 1519. In this sense, European settlers could view conquest as a means to a just end. The European project was to take corrective measures that would cultivate or civilize indigenous peoples. If implementation of these measures required taking control of natural resources (land) and the people themselves (labour), then so be it.

Globalization

Europe's industrialization and the expansion of international trade changed the landscape facing anyone who sustained himself or herself by labour alone in the 19th century. Landless workers, who no longer grew their own food, were increasingly dependent on markets to provide them with the necessities of life such as food and clothing. Workers' demand for food, clothing, and household goods stimulated specialization in production. Commerce negotiated through market exchanges moved to the centre of workers' lives. Wages from labour provided access to the market. This phenomenon affected workers across countries. Job loss and a descent into poverty could occur due to circumstances on the other side of the globe and hence far beyond the control of an individual worker.

Industrialization and the expansion of international trade presented a more generalized form of risk of impoverishment within populations. This risk provided Western governments with a compelling rationale for a broad response. It was in the interest of social stability that the public at large assisted people harmed by industrialization and trade, at least temporarily. The alternative was to leave them to fend for themselves where they could engage in criminal activity or worse yet, organize and protest for fundamental change such as redistribution of land, income, or wealth. This was not an attractive option for elites who wished to preserve the established social hierarchy. Thus, we began to see less punitive responses to poverty by governments in rapidly industrializing nations. A leader in this regard was Germany, with the introduction of nationwide compulsory health insurance for blue-collar workers, artisans, and some service workers in 1883. Benefits included medical care, paid leave while ill, and coverage of pharmaceuticals. Contributions from employees and employers paid for it. The German health insurance scheme provided a blueprint for 20th-century social insurance initiatives worldwide.

From the early 19th century to the early 20th century, income and wealth gaps between the West and the rest of the world grew further. The Industrial Revolution took hold in North America and Australia and international trade expanded like never before. Inventions during the Industrial Revolution such as steam-powered engines lowered the cost of moving goods and people over large distances. The telegraph and the transatlantic cable lowered the cost of communications. Starting from a base where it was already twice as wealthy as the rest of the world, Angus Maddison documents that Western Europe, North America, and Australia grew twice as fast as the rest of the world on average during this century. While clearly beneficial for economic growth worldwide in an absolute sense, this first wave of globalization left vast regions of the world like Latin America, the Middle East, South and East Asia, and sub-Saharan Africa behind. Thus, in a relative sense, the rest of the world was poorer. Why?

Economic historian Jeffrey Williamson argues that globalization actually encouraged deindustrialization and rising inequality within countries that traded with the rapidly industrializing countries of Western Europe, North America, and Australia. Increased demand for primary products as inputs into industrial production processes raised the price of primary goods relative to other goods. Regions capable of producing primary products responded to higher prices for them by shifting domestic production towards primary products and away from industry. Other things being equal, greater sales of primary products could have led to general prosperity for primary producing regions. The organization of production in these regions, however, prevented broad-based shared prosperity. Land ownership was highly concentrated. Politically powerful landowners were in a position to suppress labour compensation. Greater income inequality and increased risk of living in poverty for labourers were the outcomes. In Chapter 7, we will have more to say about how severe income inequality impedes shared prosperity.

Precursors to modern anti-poverty programmes

A worldwide economic depression, a near complete collapse of the international monetary system, a sharp decline in world trade, and World War II brought the first half of the 20th century to a close. The Great Depression of the 1930s was a prolonged and deep contraction in industrial production. In response to this contraction, firms reduced employment. In Western Europe, North America, and Australia, the unemployment rate topped 20 per cent during the Great Depression. The high level of unemployment led to widespread misery in industrial countries. Because of the contraction in economic activity and high unemployment, demand for primary products declined. The resulting collapse in trade transmitted the contraction in economic activity to trading partners of industrialized countries, including countries specializing in primary goods exports. It is somewhat ironic that the demands of warfare provided, in part, the economic stimulus needed to pull the world economy out of depression. Firms needed workers and new machines to produce armaments on a large scale. Further, countries needed men to populate armies. Thus, labour surpluses of the 1930s evaporated quickly in the early 1940s. In the immediate aftermath of World War II, however, there remained large-scale destruction of housing and productive equipment, and displaced populations throughout Europe. More broadly, a return to the Gold Standard, a monetary system where in principle someone could exchange a unit of a nation's currency for a fixed amount of gold, was untenable and the world trading system was in a shambles.

In response to the mass unemployment of the 1930s and the turmoil of World War II and its aftermath, governments in industrialized countries became more active at the national level and more cooperative at the international level in the struggle against poverty. Examples of this activism and cooperation were President Franklin Delano Roosevelt's (FDR) New Deal in the United States and the establishment of the World Bank (more formally, the International Bank for Reconstruction and Development) and the International Monetary Fund (IMF) in 1944 at the United Nations Monetary and Financial Conference at Bretton Woods, New Hampshire, in the United States.

The signature programme in FDR's New Deal was Social Security, which began in 1935. A goal of Social Security was to break the tight link between poverty and old age. Before Social Security, for many elderly Americans, retirement meant a life of poverty. Private pensions were rare. If family and friends were not able to provide support, then retired workers were on their own once their personal savings ran out. Social Security provided some protection to retirees against the risk of outliving one's personal savings. Eventually, the government expanded its coverage to other people at risk of poverty such as the disabled and survivors of insured workers. Building on the German model, Social Security was a form of social insurance. Mandatory contributions from employees and employers funded it. Individuals paid into the system while they were working and received payments from the system once they retired.

As World War II ended, it was clear that no country in Europe was able to finance its own reconstruction and much less to address the deprivation facing populations worldwide. International cooperation was required. Bretton Woods established the World Bank to lend funds to countries for specific projects that would foster reconstruction and spur long-term development. Member states' contributions, interest charges on its loans, and returns on its market investments fund the World Bank. Bretton Woods established the IMF to enhance international macroeconomic stability. It provides advice about macroeconomic policy. It also provides short-term bridge loans to countries that are in critical situations with respect to their indebtedness to other countries. Member states' contributions, interest charges on its loans, and its gold holdings fund the IMF.

In the post-World War II period, the effectiveness of the IMF's and World Bank's responses to countries in crisis proved controversial. The IMF and World Bank would sometimes mandate that indebted and distressed countries enact austerity measures (restraints on public spending, for example) as a condition for receiving loans from them. Austerity in the midst of crisis could make economic recovery more difficult. Critics have argued that the IMF's and World Bank's structural adjustment programmes exacerbated the situation facing distressed countries and made graduation out of poverty more difficult for their citizens. Any assessment of such arguments would require the ability to count the number of people living in poverty at a given point in time as well as over time. Thus, the presence of these organizations catalysed the analytical effort to measure poverty systematically and on a large scale.

Chapter 3
Measurement

Questions for measurement

In Chapter 2, we saw that the desire to assess anti-poverty policies of governments and international organizations stimulated the effort to measure poverty systematically. This effort required answers to basic questions that arose when attempting to document progress against poverty: What do we mean when we say someone is living in poverty? Do we mean that their income is too low, that their consumption is too low, or that given their particular level of either, their ability to participate in society is severely restricted? Once a poverty line is set, other questions arise. Should our focus be on individuals or families? Should non-monetary benefits that people receive count towards making them less impoverished? For public policy purposes, we need simple statistics that summarize the state of affairs overall. What percentage of the population is living in poverty? Only by tracking such statistics over time can we determine whether our efforts to reduce poverty are paying dividends.

Measures of well-being

Income is widely used as a measure of well-being. A high income provides a family or household with a greater command over goods and services than a low income, other things being equal.

We measure income from surveys of the population. Large random samples of the population provide a basis for constructing a nation's income distribution. A difficulty, however, is that some people are reluctant to report their income accurately. Therefore, even when national statistical agencies use sophisticated sampling and survey techniques, there is likely to be some error in measuring income. This problem may be especially acute at lower and upper ends of the income distribution.

Consumption is also a leading measure of well-being. The reason is that income may be an imperfect measure of what people are ultimately able to consume. For example, extended family members or friends may give resources to a household permitting it to consume goods and services even when its own income is low. Statistical agencies also measure consumption expenditures from surveys. Total consumption expenditures at the household level, however, do not necessarily fully capture actual consumption of the household. Consumption also includes the flow of services from durable goods such as housing. For example, a house provides its inhabitants with services such as protection from the weather. It also provides space to rear children, share meals, celebrate holidays, and park vehicles. These housing services need not have associated with them current expenditures on housing. National statistical agencies use imputation methods to account for the flow of services from durable goods. That is, they attempt to estimate the value of, say, services you derive from your home each month by observing how much it would cost you to rent a comparable home for a month. Another issue that can arise when using consumption as a measure of well-being is the interpretation of consumption of medical care. If consumption of medical care rises due to poor health, is an individual better off?

Wealth, or a stock of assets, has a special quality. It can provide access to goods and services without incurring a trade-off between work and leisure in the current period. If I do not have any wealth, then in order to consume I have to work and earn income. I can then use that income to buy goods and services that I would like to consume. For every hour I work, I have one less hour to enjoy leisure. If I have a stock of assets (wealth) to draw upon, however, I will derive income from interest earnings on those assets. Alternatively, I could sell some of my assets so that I have cash on hand. Either alternative provides me with resources to buy goods and services without having to give up leisure.

While recognition of wealth's role as a gauge of well-being is high, in practice its use in the measurement of poverty is not as prominent as income or consumption. The reasons are straightforward. First, there are challenges in measuring wealth from surveys among people at the lower end of the income distribution. For example, they may not want to disclose their savings due to mistrust. Additionally, they may hold any wealth they have outside of the formal financial sector. Therefore, they may misreport their wealth due to informal record keeping. Second, the thought that living in poverty is consistent with positive levels of asset holdings may be disconcerting.

These reservations notwithstanding, the study of asset holdings among people living in poverty is increasing. Why? Because people living in poverty are concerned with the same issues as people with higher incomes. They must figure out how much to save and in what form to store that saving. They care about the liquidity of their assets. They care about whether their assets can be stored safely. Finally, they care about the rate of return on their assets. When you think about it, the commonality of these concerns across income groups makes sense. People living in poverty face considerable uncertainty about availability of work and continuity of income. Saving for lean times can be the key to surviving those periods. The amount of savings may be small but its role in preserving household well-being is no less vital.

A capable critique

There is more to well-being than command over goods and services, however. Amartya Sen and Martha Nussbaum, among others, argue that traditional resource-based measures of well-being, such as income, are deficient because they do not capture qualitative aspects of well-being such as life expectancy, infant mortality, and educational opportunity. The capabilities approach, for which they are proponents, recognizes these aspects of well-being explicitly. This approach moves beyond purely economic measures such as income and wealth to those that more directly capture qualitative aspects of well-being. For example, in sub-Saharan Africa in 2015, the infant mortality rate, measured as the number of deaths among live children less than one year of age per 1,000 live births, was fifty-six compared to thirty-two in the rest of the world according to the World Bank. As a way of thinking about development, the capabilities approach would give as much weight to the question of how to reduce the infant mortality rate in sub-Saharan Africa as to the question of how to raise per capita income in that region. To take another example, if an individual does not have access to quality healthcare and education, then she would have difficulty participating fully in society. From the perspective of capabilities, what you are able to do matters just as much as the resources you have. This way of thinking redirects our attention to ensuring that each individual has the resources necessary to live a life of purpose, meaning, and fulfilment.

Society plays a role in providing individuals with the opportunity to pursue a good life. In some cases, creating these opportunities is more about removing social barriers than it is about providing financial resources directly. In Chapter 7, we discuss how some societies restrict the activities of women and girls thereby limiting their ability to learn, work, play, and to express themselves. To hold society accountable for these deficits, it would be advantageous to measure broadly how society is doing with regard to access to qualitative dimensions of well-being that make people capable of functioning in a meaningful way.

Inspired by the capabilities approach, the United Nation's Human Development Index (HDI) does this. The HDI summarizes well-being along three dimensions: life expectancy, years of schooling, and per capita income. The HDI is available for over 180 countries. We classify each country into one of four categories: very high human development, high human development, medium human development, and low human development. Table 5 shows the top three countries in each HDI category in 2014. The capabilities approach ensures our sobriety as we discuss standard measures of poverty. We know that there are inherent shortcomings in any purely resource-based measure. We proceed in our discussion of them with these shortcomings fully in mind.

Table 5 Human Development Index rankings

Very high human development	High human development
(1) Norway	(50) Belarus
(2) Australia	(50) Russian Federation
(3) Switzerland	(52) Oman
Medium human development	**Low human development**
(106) Botswana	(145) Kenya
(107) Moldova	(146) Nepal
(108) Egypt	(147) Pakistan

N.B. The numbers in parentheses are country rank worldwide. For example, Belarus and Russia tied for 50th place in the HDI ranking in 2014.

Source: Human Development Report Office, United Nations Development Programme: hdr.undp.org. used under Creative Commons license 3.0 http://hdr.undp.org/en/content/copyright-and-terms-use. Data taken from the 2015 Human Development Report (page 208): http://hdr.undp.org/sites/default/files/2015_human_development_report_1.pdf

Setting the poverty line: local

Suppose we select income as society's measure of well-being. A poverty line (or threshold) is an amount of income per unit of time (for example, a year) that a household would have to surpass for us not to classify its members as living in poverty.

A poverty line is absolute if it does not change as society's distribution of income shifts over time. We construct an absolute poverty line from the bottom up. The bottom in this context is the amount of food needed to prevent starvation. That amount of food costs a certain amount of money. If we are considering minimums for a productive life, then it seems that a poverty line set just at the level of income required to prevent starvation would be too low. An alternative is to consider nutrition more broadly and to consider the annual cost of a basic diet that would permit adults to be productive workers and children to grow at normal rates. This would cause us to set the poverty line a little higher. Because there is more to well-being than food intake, however, there is scope for considering other necessities, like clothing and shelter, and their costs. Doing so would cause us to set the poverty line higher still. A consensus about what necessities to include in the bundle of goods and services permits us to establish a poverty line based on the cost of that bundle.

In practice, governments conduct surveys of households' income and consumption patterns. We use data from these surveys to calculate the share of total expenditures spent on food, clothing, and other items. When we combine the cost of a basic nutritional diet with knowledge of the share of total expenditure spent on food, it is possible to calculate a total level of expenditure (and hence income) required to achieve a basic level of well-being: the absolute poverty line. Over time, we adjust this poverty line to keep pace with inflation so that command over goods and services that constitute the bundle remains constant. Many developing countries use an absolute poverty line. The United States is exceptional because it is a high-income country with an absolute poverty line.

A poverty line is relative if it changes as society's distribution of income shifts over time. A relative poverty line embeds the notion that full participation in society requires additional resources as society as a whole becomes richer. We construct a relative poverty line from the top down. The top in this context is median household income (or consumption) of a society. A household at median income has the capacity to enjoy essential activities, such as education and civic engagement, associated with citizenship in addition to providing for basic needs (food, clothing, and shelter). Social norms can develop around the level of participation in society that earning median income affords. What is the minimum fraction of median income required to have access to a reasonable amount of the social norms that society provides? Here, we define reasonable as sufficient for people to feel that they are included as a part of the society in which they live as opposed to feeling as though they are on its fringes or outside of it. Is that fraction 60 per cent of median income or will 50 per cent of median income do the job? Societies that deploy a relative poverty line have taken a stand on this question.

Many high-income countries set their poverty line to a fraction of median income. As median income rises, the poverty line rises with it. European Union (EU) countries, for example, set their national poverty lines to 60 per cent of median disposable (i.e. after-tax) income where this income also includes transfer payments that people receive directly from the government due to disability, unemployment, and old age.

In the EU, however, we subsume poverty status under a broader concept: at risk of poverty or social exclusion (AROPE). AROPE means that a household is living in at least one of three conditions: income is below the national poverty line; there is severe material deprivation; or a household has very low work intensity. Severe material deprivation is present when a household lacks sufficient resources to afford a subset of a prescribed list of basic goods including a television, a car, a meal with protein every other day, and home heating. Very low work intensity is present when adults in a household worked less than 20 per cent of the time that they could have worked during the previous twelve months.

Setting the poverty line: global

Countries set their national poverty lines based on domestic conceptions of what it means to live in poverty. This practice raises the possibility that we could classify individuals with the same level of material well-being as living in poverty simply because they reside in one country as opposed to another. Under these circumstances, it would be difficult to attach meaning to a calculation that summed the number of people living in poverty using counts from multiple countries because we could classify similarly situated individuals differently. To avoid possible confusion, an effort has been underway at the World Bank since 1990 to construct a global poverty line. We derive a global poverty line from the national poverty lines of several of the world's poorest countries. Calculation of a global poverty line requires that we standardize and then average national poverty lines.

Purchasing power parity (PPP) tells us the number of units of one nation's currency we would need to purchase a representative basket of goods and services valued in the units of another nation's currency. Suppose it is possible to construct in each country a basket of goods and services of exactly the same quality and quantity. For the sake of simplicity, let us assume that this basket is representative of the consumption preferences of the typical household in each country and that the typical household is the same in each country. We trade some of the goods and services in the basket internationally but do not trade others of them on international markets. We ask ourselves: 'How much does this basket of goods and services cost in each nation in terms of its own currency?' If we weight the price of each good and service in the basket by its share of total expenditure on the basket as a whole and sum the weighted prices, then we would have calculated the (weighted) average price of the basket. Suppose we conducted this exercise for every country in the world. Then, we chose one currency to serve as the base or numeraire. In practice, the US dollar serves as the numeraire currency. We could then rescale the average prices of all of the other countries by dividing the average price of the basket in units of their national currency by the average price of the basket in units of the numeraire currency. The result is PPP. Notice that the units of PPP are the ratio of national currency to numeraire currency. Therefore, PPP is essentially a special kind of exchange rate.

The World Bank's International Comparison Program calculates PPP for almost every country in the world. The World Bank collaborates with national governments to conduct surveys that record the prices of several hundred goods and services in each country. To the extent possible, the surveys standardize the list of goods and services recorded and account for differences in the quality of products across countries.

The global poverty line is an absolute poverty line. It is the average of national poverty lines of a set of the poorest countries in the world all expressed in PPP dollars (PPP$). In 1990, the World Bank announced that this average was approximately PPP$1 a day. At that time, 'a dollar a day' served as the benchmark for extreme poverty at the global level. In 2015, the World Bank updated the benchmark for extreme poverty to PPP$1.90 a day. There is, however, nothing intrinsically special about the approximately two dollar a day threshold. Currently, the number of people living in poverty can be calculated using different global poverty lines at the World Bank's website. Table 1 and Table 2 in Chapter 1 show trends in global poverty over time using the PPP\$1.90 a day poverty line.

We summarize the worldwide count of people living below the PPP\$1.90 a day poverty line by regional aggregations of the country totals. The regions are East Asia and Pacific, Eastern Europe and Central Asia, Latin America and the Caribbean, Middle East and North Africa, South Asia, and sub-Saharan Africa. Typically, we do not include high-income countries such as those in North America and Western Europe in the count or summary. As shown in Table 2, most of the extreme poverty in the world is concentrated in three regions: sub-Saharan Africa, South Asia, and East Asia and Pacific.

Counting resources

Whom we count as living in poverty depends on the unit of observation in addition to where we set the poverty line. Is the unit of observation a household, a family, or an individual? A household is individuals living together without regard to familial relationship between them. This unit is relevant because household members are able to share resources. A family is individuals that are directly related, living together, and sharing resources. An individual is someone living alone. The unit of observation matters because it should be consistent with the poverty threshold. It answers the question, *whose* resources (per unit of time) should we add together for comparison to the poverty threshold. For example, if we select the household as the unit of observation and say the time frame is one year, then we sum the income of all members of the household over the course of a year. Then, we compare that sum to the relevant threshold. If the ratio of household income to the threshold is less than one, then we classify all members of the household as living in poverty. Notice that if we shifted the unit of observation in this example to the family, then the sum of incomes could be different because we would exclude the income of unrelated individuals. It is possible that we would reach a different conclusion about the poverty status of family members when we compare family income to a poverty threshold based on family units.

Households come in different sizes. How do we establish an absolute poverty line that represents approximately equal levels of well-being across households with different numbers of members? The members of a large household with a given income will not be as well off as members of a smaller household with the same income. An adjustment to the poverty threshold that recognizes that a larger household needs a larger income to be as well off as a smaller household with a similar income is required.

The relevant adjustment, however, should account for efficiencies in consumption. That is, should a household double in size, it does not need to double its resources to maintain the level of well-being of each member of the household. The reason is that it is possible to share resources that provide consumption services. An example is a kitchen. As a household grows, family members can still use a single kitchen in the home to prepare meals for everyone. Equivalence scales make these adjustments.

A well-known equivalence scale is $\sqrt{N}$ where N is the number of members in the household. Suppose that two households are compared, one with $N = 4$ and the other with $N = 1$. Clearly, the first household is four times as large as the second. Because of efficiencies in consumption, however, the first household's income need not be four times as large for members of this household to be as well off as the single member of the second household. Rather, the equivalence scale indicates that the first household's income only needs to be double ($\sqrt{4} = 2$) that of the second household's income to provide the same level of well-being. A more complicated equivalence scale would also account for the view that children consume less than adults on average would. An example from the National Academy of Sciences in the US is

$\sqrt{(A + 0.5C)}$ where A is the number of adults and C is the number of children in the household.

Taxes and transfers

We must also make a decision about *what* resources to count against the threshold in order to determine who is living in poverty. Should we count income before or after taxes? Should we count the value of in-kind benefits from the government as income? Should we subtract expenses for necessities such as transportation and medical out-of-pocket expenses from the measure of resources? Answers to these kinds of questions impact the sums calculated and the classification of who is living in poverty. In high-income countries, these questions are the subject of ongoing study and debate.

High-income countries have well-developed tax and transfer systems. Households pay taxes on income. Some households may receive transfers from the government. Transfers can be in the form of cash payments or they may be in kind. In-kind transfers provide people with access to goods and services without receipt of cash from the government. An example of an in-kind transfer programme in the United States is the Supplemental Nutrition Assistance Program, known more widely as the 'food stamps' programme, which provides people living in poverty with access to qualifying foodstuffs. In France, the social security (*sécurité sociale*) system provides health services.

We can also use the tax system to boost income received from working and thereby reduce poverty. That may be surprising because we do not typically think of the tax system as adding to our income. Perhaps it is more helpful to think of the imposition of a negative income tax. The Earned Income Tax Credit (EITC) in the United States is a conditional tax credit. The EITC increases the return to working by providing a credit against taxes owed. It pays cash to a worker if the credit is greater than

4. Earned Income Tax Credit.

the amount of taxes owed. It is available on the condition that eligible individuals work.

Figure 4 shows the structure of the EITC for a single parent with one child in 2016. The numbers are in thousands of US dollars (\$). The EITC has a phase-in range, \$0 to \$9,900, during which the credit increases with earnings. Once the credit reaches its maximum, \$3,373, the credit is constant as earnings increase. Finally, there is a phase-out range, \$18,200 to \$39,300, during which the credit declines as earnings increase. The EITC is also available for married couples with dependent children. The EITC for workers without dependent children is extremely modest; a maximum credit of \$506 per annum in 2016. The EITC is relevant only for workers with low to moderate annual earnings. We discuss the EITC further in Chapter 5 in the context of the labour market.

In the United Kingdom, we have the Working Tax Credit and the Child Tax Credit. A single worker with one child must work at least sixteen hours per week to be eligible for the Working Tax Credit. In 2016, such a worker could receive up to £2,010 from this programme. The Child Tax Credit is an unconditional benefit. It does not have a work requirement. Any adult responsible for care of a child is eligible to receive this benefit. In 2016, such an adult could receive up to £2,780 from this programme. These programmes do not have sharp income cut-offs like the EITC in the US because they take into consideration other factors such as childcare costs. Further, these programmes are in transition, as the UK's Universal Credit (UC) introduced in 2013 will eventually subsume both of them. The UC is a single monthly payment for people over 18 but not receiving a pension, working, or unemployed, and with savings of less than £16,000. The government augments the payment in support of children and housing expenses. There is a cap on the total annual payment from the programme, as well as a phase-out provision. As annual earnings rise, the payment falls.

Developing countries have less well-developed tax and transfer systems. Nevertheless, a number of these countries have cash transfer programmes. These programmes provide regularly timed stipends to some of the poorest members of society. There are two types of programmes: conditional cash transfers and unconditional cash transfers. In conditional cash transfer programmes, receipt of the stipend is contingent on completion of prescribed actions such as school attendance by children in the household or presentation of children for vaccination. In unconditional cash transfer programmes, the government gives a stipend without conditions attached. Cash transfers count against the poverty threshold with the express goal of combating poverty.

The Jawtno Program in Bangladesh is an example of a conditional cash programme. This programme, a collaboration between the government of Bangladesh and the World Bank, pays cash to pregnant women and mothers if they engage in activities that promote nutrition and growth of their children aged 0–5 years old. These activities include regular prenatal care visits, monitoring of child growth, and nutrition counselling. To be eligible for the programme, household income must be in the bottom 40 per cent of the income distribution and children must be less than 5 years old. The cash payment is the equivalent of approximately $15 per month. The Jawtno Program launched officially in 2017 although it is actually a scaling up of the Shombhob pilot programme that began in 2011. The Shombhob pilot provided evidence that a conditional cash programme could improve child nutrition and child growth outcomes in Bangladesh where children are at increased risk of illness and disease related to malnutrition. In Chapter 7, we discuss how we use randomized control trials to establish the effectiveness of anti-poverty interventions like the Shombhob.

Poverty gaps

Once rules have been determined for classifying individuals as living in poverty or not, it is possible to devise summary statistics that answer questions that are relevant for public policy. For example, how pervasive is poverty in society? The headcount index, more popularly known as the poverty rate, provides an answer to this question. Its definition is the number of people living in poverty divided by the population. We measure each component of this ratio per unit of time, typically one year. The headcount index measures the *incidence* of poverty within a given population.

While the definition of the headcount ratio is straightforward, the measurement of its components can be subject to refinement. For example, the denominator, the count of the population, may exclude individuals who are institutionalized (prisoners, military personnel, students, and senior citizens) because we do not link their overall well-being directly to their participation in market-based transactions and outcomes. The numerator excludes all members of households whose household income is even one dollar above the relevant poverty threshold. The well-being of members of such a household may not be materially different from members of a household classified as living in poverty. This point is salient when it comes to public policy. If a large number of households are just below the poverty line, then policymakers have an incentive to enact public policies that move them just above the poverty line. A potential pay-off of such a policy could be a noticeable reduction in measured poverty without much improvement in overall well-being. This is a drawback of the headcount index.

Society might care about more than just the number of people classified as living in poverty. A significant share of households could be very poor (viz., their incomes are far below the poverty line) while a much smaller share of households is just below the poverty line. The appropriate public policies for such a society could be quite different from an alternative society where a significant share of households is just below the poverty line while a much smaller share of households is very poor. Therefore, it would be convenient to have measures that characterize the *depth* and *severity* of poverty for the representative household. In the early 1980s, the economist James Foster and his collaborators figured out how to do this.

For a household classified as living in poverty, the difference between its income and the relevant poverty threshold is the gap in resources required to lift it out of poverty. If we divide this gap by the threshold, the resulting ratio yields the resources required to lift the household out of poverty as a percentage of the poverty threshold. Suppose that we calculate this ratio for every household classified as living in poverty. The average of all of the ratios is a measure of the depth of poverty on average. It tells us the amount of resources required as a percentage of the poverty thresholds to lift the representative household out of poverty.

One approach to characterizing the severity of poverty is to modify slightly the calculation of the gap ratios described in the previous paragraph. That modification is to square the gap ratios before averaging them across the poverty population. Households whose incomes are farther below their poverty threshold are likely to be worse off than households whose incomes are just slightly below their poverty threshold. Therefore, it would be useful to give more weight to large gaps in the calculation of a single index value thought to summarize the degree of poverty in a society. The squaring effectively gives more weight to large deviations from the poverty thresholds. Large values of this modified index indicate that the degree of poverty is very severe.

Accountability

Fundamentally, statistics, head counts, and surveys offer a way of measuring poverty. Measurement is crucial because it provides a mechanism for holding ourselves accountable to each other. The public has a right to know whether resources spent to alleviate poverty are achieving that goal. If they are not, then the public can ask policymakers why. To do that, the public needs documentation about poverty at regular time intervals in a format that is comparable over time. This is where measurement comes in and why we care about it. In Chapter 2, we discussed criticisms levelled at the World Bank and the IMF for policies that required fiscal austerity in the face of economic hardship. Data on the despair experienced by people buttressed critics' arguments. Professionals who grappled with many of the issues discussed in this chapter collected, curated, and published those data.

We will also see that careful measurement extends our understanding of the contextual nature of poverty. In Chapter 1, we contrasted the kitchens of people living in poverty in different parts of the world. In Chapter 4, we consider the contextual nature of other dimensions of well-being.

Chapter 4
Living: here and there

Five dimensions that affect well-being

What it means to live in poverty depends on where in the world you are. In Chapter 1, we illustrated this point by considering the features of a basic kitchen. Here, we compare and contrast five additional dimensions of life that underpin our notion of well-being: family structure, health, education, assets, and the environment. Our focus is on qualitative characteristics that seem to persist over time, although some data are included in order to provide broader context.

Family structure

A family's structure dictates the everyday living arrangements of its members. Some families are large; some are small. Some families have dependent children; others do not. In some families, there are two or more adults, in others only one adult. The potential configurations are endless. As discussed in Chapter 3, there is also a distinction between a family and a household. That distinction recognizes that people living together may be unrelated biologically, but they share resources and live under the same roof. They are a household.

In developed countries, poverty is strongly associated with a single parent raising a child or children alone. From household surveys in the EU conducted in 2015, we know that the AROPE rate was 48 per cent for a single parent with dependent children while it was only 17.6 per cent for households with two adults and one dependent child. More than one in four (26.9 per cent) children (aged 17 years or younger) in the EU are AROPE. In the United States, official poverty rates by family structure in 2015 exhibit the same pattern: 38 per cent for a single parent with dependent children, but only 11.7 per cent for two-parent families with one dependent child. Overall, one in five children in the US lives in poverty.

In Chapter 6, we consider events that trigger periods of poverty. Dissolution of the family unit (through bereavement or relationship breakdown, for example) is one of those triggers, especially when there are dependent children. Not only are there fewer financial resources in single-parent families, there is also less time for parenting. Single parents have less time to schedule and attend preventative healthcare appointments for children; to shop and prepare nutritious meals; or to do homework and enrichment activities with their children. Scarcity of parental time can lead to a decline in the health, educational attainment, and well-being of children.

In the United States, the poverty rate for female-headed families with dependent children was 40 per cent in 2015. For male-headed families with dependent children, it was 22 per cent for that same year. The disparity in these poverty rates emerged in the 1970s and has persisted since then. Social scientists call this disparity the feminization of poverty. It has a multitude of causes. First, there may be discrimination against women in the labour market. If women do not receive equal pay for equal work, then households headed by them will have fewer resources with which to manage. Second, society may channel women into occupations that do not pay well. Low-paying occupations effectively cap earnings at levels that may be insufficient to make ends meet. Third, workplace norms may not easily accommodate disruptions in female labour supply due to childbirth and child rearing. Such norms can compromise the career trajectory of women. Fourth, women do a disproportionate amount of the unpaid care work in society, which reduces their time available for paid work. These reasons connect with the challenges facing women and girls more generally in their struggle to graduate out of poverty, as discussed in Chapter 7 in more detail.

In the developing country context, poverty is associated with adults living together with dependent children. In sub-Saharan Africa (excluding South Africa) and India, approximately 50 per cent of children live with extended family (other adults in addition to parents). Such living arrangements allow pooling of financial resources and can create efficiencies with respect to child rearing. A large family size can result from an extended family living together or from a high fertility rate (the average number of children born to each woman of childbearing age) or from a combination of the two. According to the World Bank, the average fertility rate is four children per woman in low-income countries (annual per capita income of $1,045 or less) as a whole. In sub-Saharan Africa, however, Niger, Mali, Burundi, and Somalia have fertility rates of six or more while Uganda, Burkina Faso, Zambia, Malawi, Angola, South Sudan, Mozambique, and Nigeria have fertility rates of five or more. In India, the fertility rate is 2.5. These high fertility rates suggest that those living in poverty in the developing world are relatively young on average. In low-income countries, 43 per cent of the population were 14 years old or younger in 2016. This compares to only 17 per cent of the population in this age range in high-income countries in the same year. As we will see when we discuss health, however, another reason why people in developing countries are young on average is that they do not live as long as people in developed countries do.

A large family is a form of insurance in developing countries. It is a source of workers, income, and childcare. It also provides support in old age, as younger generations take care of older ones.

Beyond economic considerations, a large family enriches its members because of shared experiences of ceremonies, festivals, faith, communal traditions, and rituals. In the absence of a social safety net, a large family sustains well-being and life. As countries strive to develop economically, however, constraining population growth and thereby altering the traditional structure of families is often one of the first coordinated public policy initiatives.

China's one-child policy from 1979 to 2015, for example, limited couples to one child. Implementation of this policy coincided with spectacular growth rates in per capita income in China. Advocates for such policies emphasize the advantages of increasing the quality of life for each child as opposed to maximizing the quantity of children. Healthier and better-educated children are more likely to earn their way out of poverty and thereby thwart intergenerational transmission of poverty. Critics of such policies note demographic imbalances in China that will have implications for future generations. According to the United Nations, China's sex ratio at birth (male births per one hundred female births) was 107 in 1980, not that unlike the world as a whole at 106. In 2015, that ratio was 116 in China, compared to 107 for the world as whole. In 2015, the sex ratio of the total population (males per one hundred females) in China was 106, compared to 102 in the world as a whole. Relatively speaking, there are too few women in China. The one-child policy induced a preference for boys. Gender imbalance, however, exposes society to risks such as uncertain marriage and fertility patterns, fierce competition for mates, fewer children in the next generation, and thereby fewer people to support the elderly in future generations.

Health

If you were born in Malawi in 1995, you could expect to live forty-three years. If you were born in Malawi in 2015, you could expect to live sixty-four years. Over a period of twenty years, Malawi managed to add twenty years to its life expectancy. How did Malawi, a low-income country, achieve such a dramatic increase? According to the World Health Organization, total health expenditures (public + private) per person per year in Malawi rose from $22 (2011 PPP$) in 1995 to $93 (2011 PPP$) in 2014. Malawi's government undertook multiple public health initiatives, including implementation of a health sector strategic plan. To combat HIV/AIDS, it expanded testing, counselling, and anti-retroviral therapy. It built health clinics and housing units for healthcare providers in rural areas so that people living there had access to care. It emphasized vaccination and immunization of children. It implemented education campaigns to promote safe sex to reduce the incidence of sexually transmitted diseases. It paid cash transfers to families with at-risk children to cover expenses related to medical or psychological care. It provided mosquito nets and insecticide spraying to reduce the incidence of malaria. It provided water purification tablets and offered education promoting personal hygiene. This more than quadrupling of health expenditures contributed to the improvement in life expectancy in Malawi.

No one can take sixty-four years of life for granted. For a low-income country, a life expectancy of sixty-four years is very good. Compared to a life expectancy of eighty-four years in Japan, a high-income country, however, the life expectancy in Malawi is less impressive.

Table 6 shows trends in three barometers of health: life expectancy, infant mortality, and stunting. Life expectancy is a key measure of health and well-being because time is the ultimate constraint on human activity. Of course, we care about years of healthy life but a short life will surely curtail these! The infant mortality rate tells us about the well-being of mother and child. If the mother was well nourished and received prenatal care, then her child will be stronger than would otherwise be the case. A stronger child has a better chance of reaching her first birthday. The prevalence of stunting is the percentage of children under five who are severely under the average height for their age. Stunting

Table 6 Health spending and health indicators by country income levels

Country group	Health expenditure (per capita, 2011 PPP$)		Life expectancy (years)		Infant mortality (deaths per 1,000 live births)		Stunting prevalence (% affected, children aged 0–5 years)	
	1995	2014	1995	2015	1995	2015	1995	2015
World	481	1,272	66	72	60	32	36	23
Low income	32	91	50	62	104	53	51	37
Middle income	138	577	65	71	60	30	39	23
High income	2,071	5,193	76	81	8	5	4	3

N.B. The health expenditure data end in 2014.

Source: The World Bank.

tells us that a child did not receive proper nutrition early in life when cognitive development is most rapid. Nutritional deficiencies in early childhood can reverberate forward because of cognitive delays that disrupt learning and skill acquisition.

Table 6 also shows annual health expenditures per person. These expenditures are the sum of public and private health expenditures as a ratio of total population. For comparability, the health expenditure figures are in 2011 PPP dollars as discussed in Chapter 3. Some care is required in interpreting Table 6 because over time a country can move from one country group to another due to growth. We focus on a time span that is long enough to indicate trends but short enough to minimize this composition effect.

The first row of Table 6 tells us that, worldwide, we are spending more on health over time. That increase in expenditure correlates positively with better health worldwide as measured by longer life expectancy, lower infant mortality, and less stunting. There is no simple story that explains differences in health outcomes across countries by income. The last three rows of Table 6, however, indicate that as income rises, spending on health also rises. This additional spending correlates with improved health outcomes. Table 6 suggests that, from a global perspective, people living in poverty experience worse health because spending on their healthcare is relatively low.

The aggregations in Table 6 mask disparities within country income groups. Looking within country income groups reveals another factor that can generate health disparities: access to healthcare. Table 7 shows trends in life expectancy, infant mortality, and health expenditures in four high-income countries. The level of spending on health in the US is exceptional. Health outcomes in the US are less so. For example, at six (per 1,000 births), the infant mortality rate in the US is higher than in many other developed nations. In Finland, the infant mortality rate is

Table 7 Health spending and health indicators in four high-income countries

Country	Health expenditure (per capita, 2011 PPP$)		Life expectancy (years)		Infant mortality (deaths per 1,000 live births)	
	1995	2014	1995	2015	1995	2015
United States	3,788	9,403	76	79	8	6
United Kingdom	1,350	3,377	77	82	6	4
Finland	1,480	3,701	76	81	4	2
France	2,102	4,508	78	83	5	4

N.B. The health expenditure data end in 2014.

Source: The World Bank.

just two (per 1,000 births). Health researchers such as Emily Oster and her collaborators found that an important driver of this difference is post-neonatal (1–12 months) deaths of children in households with low socio-economic status. In the US, living in poverty is associated with a higher infant mortality rate. Moreover, this association is stronger the greater the depth of income poverty experienced by a child's household. The infant mortality rate for households living at less than 50 per cent of the poverty line is higher than the infant mortality rate of households living at 50 per cent to 100 per cent of the poverty line. Poverty is also positively associated with pre-term (< 37 weeks of gestation) births and low birth weight (< 2,500 grams). Further, the high level of spending is not purchasing more years of life. As Table 7 indicates, life expectancy in the US is lower than in other high-income countries that spend much less on health.

France, Finland, and the United Kingdom provide universal access to healthcare through the public sector. Taxes finance the provision of basic care for everyone. Universal coverage decouples access to basic care from socio-economic status.

Prevention of illness is less expensive than treatment of it. Universal coverage creates the possibility that doctors can sustain preventative care even when patients' life circumstances change. For an expectant mother, for example, this means that prenatal care can continue even though she may have lost her job. Continuation of her care means that it is less likely that her child will be born prematurely or underweight. It enhances the chances that her child will live to see its first birthday, thereby reducing the rate of infant mortality.

In the US, health insurance is an employer-based benefit for employees. The private sector provides most healthcare to workers and their families. This system emerged during World War II. At that time, workers were scarce. Government wage and price controls limited workers' compensation. In the face of these regulations, employers competed for workers using non-wage mechanisms, one of which was health insurance as a benefit. In addition, the government granted this particular benefit tax-free status in 1943.

For people in the US who are poor, disabled, elderly (over 64 years of age), or veterans, health insurance is provided publically. For those same groups, the public or private sector may provide healthcare. Thus, the US has a complex hybrid system of health insurance and healthcare. Incomplete coverage is one of its hallmarks. If you are between the ages of 26 and 64 and unemployed, the probability that you have health insurance is lower. One reason for this is that you have to pay for it directly. That is difficult to do without a job because it is expensive. Also, if you have a pre-existing medical condition, private insurance companies are reluctant to insure you because you are more likely to file a claim. Therefore, while the US spends a great deal on health, access to care is uneven and inconsistent. This is one reason why health outcomes in the US are not on a par with other high-income countries.

Education

Health and education interact in at least three ways for children: physical growth, cognitive development, and school attendance. Good health is a prerequisite for learning. Like good health, education is a lever for lifting people out of poverty. It improves labour market opportunities available to individuals, improves their human capital, and helps to inform the life choices that they make. More broadly, it may enhance an individual's participation in the civic life of his or her community, thereby allowing her to feel more included.

Table 8 shows trends in three indicators of educational success: primary school enrolment and the rate at which girls and boys progress into secondary education. The net enrolment rate is the ratio of children of official school age who enrolled in school to the population of the corresponding official school age. Ideally, we would want an enrolment rate of 100 per cent, indicating that all primary school-aged children enrol in school. No set pattern exists as to where developing countries lie relative to the world average. In sub-Saharan Africa (excluding South Africa), the (net) school enrolment rate at the primary level was 77 per cent in 2014. In 2009, the Right to Education Act made school enrolment for children between 6 and 14 years old compulsory in India. In 2014, the primary school enrolment rate in India was 90 per cent. The progression rates are the percentage of children who complete their primary schooling and in the next year enrol in the first level of secondary schooling. High progression rates suggest that educational norms have surpassed the most basic (primary) level. Table 8 also shows the pupil-to-teacher ratio. This ratio is a proxy for resources available in the educational sector. It seems reasonable to associate a lower pupil-to-teacher ratio with a better-funded educational sector.

The first row of Table 8 tells us that worldwide, we are directing more resources into the educational sector over time. These

Table 8 Education indicators by country income levels

Country group	Pupil–teacher ratio		Enrolment rate (net, %)		Female progression (% enrol in secondary school)		Male progression (% enrol in secondary school)	
	1995	2014	1995	2014	1995	2013	1995	2013
World	26	24	82	89	83	91	86	91
Low income	41	43	49	80	59	76	58	78
Middle income	28	24	84	90	82	92	86	92
High income	16	14	95	96	97	97	96	97

N.B. The progression data end in 2013.

Source: The World Bank.

additional resources correlate positively with an increase in school enrolment and an increase in the rate at which girls and boys transition into higher levels of education. In education, as with health, there is no simple story that explains differences in educational outcomes across countries by income. Yet, the parallel between education and health is remarkable. The last three rows of Table 8 suggest that as income rises, spending on education also rises. This additional spending correlates with improved educational outcomes. Table 8 suggests that, from a global perspective, people living in poverty experience worse education because spending on their education is relatively low.

Table 8 also conveys that girls 'caught up' with boys in a culturally meaningful way. Comparing the columns on female and male progression, we see in the first row that boys were ahead in 1995. By 2013, however, girls and boys tied with progression rates of 91 per cent. Looking down these two columns, we see that educational gains by girls in middle-income countries are most responsible for closing this gender gap. In Chapter 7, we discuss social limitations placed on women and girls that inhibit their capacity for self-determination. Therefore, it is encouraging to note here the progress girls are making in their struggle to become educated.

Enrolment in school is one thing; learning is another thing altogether. Are children learning in school? Answers to this question are similar for people living in poverty in developed and developing country contexts.

In India, the educational experience reflects that in several developing countries. Non-governmental organizations (NGOs) such as Pratham provide education services on the ground in India and report regularly on learning outcomes there. Reading levels are below grade levels. Nearly 50 per cent of 10 and 11 year olds cannot read at the 7-year-old level. In addition, 50 per cent of 10 and 11 year olds cannot do basic maths (addition and subtraction) at the 7-year-old level. Teacher absenteeism, at about 15 per cent on any given day, makes it difficult to sustain classroom continuity. Relative to teachers in private schools, teachers in government schools are more likely to have a formal teaching degree but the percentage of children enrolled in private schools is increasing over time. Enrolment in school does not necessary imply that the child attends school regularly. In the developing country context, children have many responsibilities within and outside the household. The need to do chores, provide care, or earn income may supersede schooling. Student absenteeism on any given day can be 25 per cent or more. School facilities define the physical environment where learning takes place. There is no guarantee that features such as toilets are present. Nevertheless, an increasing percentage of schools in India do have usable toilets. Computers, library books, midday meals, and playgrounds are also becoming more common in schools.

In the US, while the details differ, the educational experience for those living in poverty is similar. Education researchers Lisa Barrow and Diane Whitmore Schanzenbach highlight many early childhood observations that influence the life chances of children living in poverty. Fourth graders (9 and 10 year olds) from households living in poverty score lower on standardized reading and maths tests than those from households who are not. They are also less likely to meet proficiency standards associated with those tests. Earlier in life, children living in poverty exhibit fewer signals associated with success in school relative to children who are not economically disadvantaged. As 9 month olds, they are less likely to explore purposefully or jabber expressively. As 2 year olds, they are less likely to use expressive vocabulary or exhibit matching discrimination. As 4 year olds, they recognize fewer letters, numbers, and shapes. Adults who grew up living in poverty are less likely to attain a Bachelor of Arts degree and it is more likely that at some point they had to repeat a grade of schooling. It is more likely that less-experienced teachers teach children living in poverty. Frequently, these teachers do not have training in the subjects they teach. As in the developing country context, health is an issue. Parents of children living in poverty are less likely to report that their child's health is excellent or very good and more likely to report that their child's health is fair or poor. They are also more likely to report that their child has a learning disability. Health issues are one cause of high rates of school absenteeism. Children living in poverty have higher absentee rates (approximately 23 per cent) than children who are not living in poverty (approximately 16 per cent). Finally, it is likely that children living in poverty attend a school with inferior classroom facilities. More likely, their classes are in temporary or portable buildings. The school is less likely to have dedicated rooms for science, art, or music instruction. School overenrolment of more than 25 per cent is more likely.

Inferior education, like inferior health, transmits poverty across generations. We know that the labour market rewards skills like reading, writing, calculation, and comprehension. These skills increase productivity that in turn leads to higher wages. Chapter 5 discusses why this is the case. We also know that children benefit directly from their parents' education. Highly educated parents expose their children to a larger vocabulary. These parents are also more likely to expose their children to extracurricular educational activities. We say more about this in Chapter 6. Because children living in poverty receive fewer incidental benefits from family members' education, some societies have introduced programmes designed to disrupt the education channel of intergenerational poverty transmission.

The United States' Head Start programme and the United Kingdom's Sure Start programme are examples of public policies designed to confront the forces of poverty that work through the education channel. Head Start started in 1965 as a part of President Lyndon B. Johnson's war on poverty. Its goal is to prepare children under 5 years old from low-income households for school by providing educational enrichment in their local community. NGOs and community groups design and implement the curriculum that students learn. The federal government funds these organizations via direct grants. The Labour Party started Sure Start in 1998. Its goal, design, implementation, and funding structure parallel those of Head Start. In Chapter 7, we describe how modern policy evaluators rigorously determine the effectiveness of programmes like Head Start and Sure Start.

Commentators and critics, however, tend to assess the cumulative effect of educational policy using a less direct, but more popular, device: international comparisons of student learning in reading, maths, and science. For example, 15 year olds in several middle-income and high-income countries take the Organization for Economic Co-operation and Development's (OECD) Program for International Student Assessment (PISA) test. Since 2000, participating countries administer the test triennially. Low-income countries do not offer the PISA because the infrastructure for administering the test is not yet in place. (India plans to offer the PISA test nationwide in 2021.)

Participating countries are keen to see how their students compare to the competition. Table 9 compares the US and the UK, two high-income countries, to Brazil and Indonesia, two middle-income countries, and the OECD average. The OECD average serves as the international standard. The international standard in reading has held steady over time, while it has declined in maths and science. The US and the UK contributed to the decline in the average OECD maths score. The UK also contributed to the decline in the average OECD science score while the US improved in science. These results are an impetus to educational reform movements in both countries. Increasing school choice for families and children living in poverty are key elements of proposed reforms. Brazil and Indonesia, on the other hand, show improvements over time in reading, maths, and science. Brazil and Indonesia started from a lower average level of skill. Nevertheless, the 15 year olds in these countries are

64

Table 9 Education trends in four countries and the OECD

Country	Reading		Maths		Science	
	2000	2015	2003	2015	2006	2015
OECD Average	493	493	499	490	498	493
United States	504	497	483	470	489	496
United Kingdom	523	498	508	492	515	509
Brazil	396	407	356	377	390	401
Indonesia	371	397	360	386	393	403

N.B. The OECD staggered the initial year of implementation: 2000 (reading), 2003 (maths), and 2006 (science). The reading, mathematics, and science scale ranges from zero to 1,000.

Source: OECD (2017), PISA test score data, <http://pisadataexplorer.oecd.org/ide/idepisa/dataset.aspx>, accessed 19 June 2017.

closing the skills gap between themselves and their counterparts in OECD countries.

Assets: financial and non-financial

A low annual income does not necessarily arrive at regular intervals. Therefore, people living in poverty attempt to smooth their consumption in the face of a fluctuating stream of income. Like their more affluent counterparts, they also try to save to pay for significant anticipated expenses such as education, business start-up, home purchase, emergencies, or even old age. Asset accumulation and holding can help them achieve these objectives. Two categories of assets are relevant. First, financial assets include various types of savings vehicles, for example, bank accounts or life insurance. Second, people living in poverty may also convert non-financial assets including land, livestock, and various durable goods into cash in an emergency. It may seem anomalous to discuss asset holdings in the context of poverty. There is ample evidence in developing county and developed country contexts, however, that some people living in poverty have modest but intricate financial lives.

The World Bank conducts surveys in developing countries in order to assess the degree of financial inclusion worldwide. It reports results of these surveys in their Global Findex Database. In low-income countries, where annual per capita income is less than $1,045, only 10 per cent of people (aged 15 years and above) have savings at a financial institution. Nevertheless, almost half (47 per cent) saved money over the course of the past year. They saved outside of financial institutions with savings clubs or with someone outside of the family. Although it is difficult to save, a positive but small percentage of people with very low incomes responded to one of three common reasons for saving: to start, operate, or expand a farm or business; for education or school fees; and for old age. In lower-middle-income countries where annual per capita income is between $1,046 and $4,125, the overall situation is parallel to that in low-income countries. A slightly higher percentage of people (15 per cent) save at a financial institution and 46 per cent saved money over the course of the past year.

We would not expect people living in extreme poverty in a developing country to possess many durable goods, but they do own some. Development economists Abhijit Banerjee and Esther Duflo document that items such as a radio and a television are more prevalent among those living on $2 a day compared to those living on $1 a day. A significant percentage of households have a bed and some have a bicycle, a clock, or a watch. If households own land, it is typically a small plot of uncertain productivity.

As a developed country, the United States provides contrast with respect to the degree of financial inclusion for people living in poverty there as opposed to a developing country. According to the US Federal Deposit Insurance Corporation, approximately half (46 per cent) of low-income families have a savings account at a financial institution. In this context, we define a low-income family as a family with an annual income of $30,000 (about $82 a day) or less. Leading reasons for opening these accounts include a safe place to put money, saving for the future, and receipt of direct deposits. About one in five of low-income families are 'unbanked', meaning that they do not have an account of any kind at a financial institution. This rate of financial exclusion is high relative to higher-income families in the US, but it is low relative to families living in poverty in low-income countries.

Households living in poverty in the United States have a number of durable goods. Surveys by US Census Bureau indicate that almost all own a television (96 per cent), a microwave oven (93 per cent), a stove (97 per cent), and a refrigerator (98 per cent). Slightly less own a cell phone (81 per cent). More than half (58 per cent) own a computer. The computer ownership rate for households not living in poverty is 81 per cent. The difference in computer ownership rates between those living in poverty and those who are not is one indicator of the digital divide in the US. Approximately one-third (32 per cent) of families living in poverty own the home where they reside. More than half (59 per cent) also own a vehicle (automobile, truck, or motorcycle). The vehicle ownership rate for households not living in poverty is 91 per cent. Thus, the vehicle ownership gap in the United States is large.

The environment

Climate change involves the observed rise in average global temperature due to emission of greenhouse gases (carbon dioxide, for example). It is also associated with an increase in the frequency and persistence of consequential weather phenomena such as floods, droughts, heat waves, rising sea levels, and wildfires. These weather phenomena disproportionately affect people living in poverty.

In the developing country context, people living in poverty rely heavily on income from farming, fishing, and tourism. Therefore, they are more exposed to the environment and financially vulnerable. In countries with high average temperatures, people living in poverty are more likely to live in areas that are hotter than average. They are also more likely to live in urban areas that are subject to flooding. They spend a larger share of their income on food. In countries where average income is low, food price spikes due to natural disasters can push people deeper into poverty. The food price spike of 2006–8 is an example. Drought condition in countries that produce soybean, wheat, and corn triggered this episode. Rapid increases in the price of food staples induces 'food insecurity' (the absence of reliable access to sufficient, good-quality food). An increase in food insecurity exacerbates pre-existing health maladies. The situation for children is especially consequential if cognitive development is impaired or stunting occurs due to undernutrition or malnutrition. Climate change could also increase the incidence of diseases such as malaria and cholera. Poor health reduces current and future earning capacity, which could lead to prolonged stints of poverty that a family transmits to the next generation.

In the developed country context, the disproportionate impact of climate change is due to many of the same reasons. In the United States, for example, those living in poverty in coastal regions along the Atlantic and Pacific Oceans, as well as the Gulf of Mexico, live in communities that are more exposed, more vulnerable, and less resilient to weather events. In areas away from the coasts, disparities are also present. People living in poverty in urban areas experience heat island effects and poor air quality. Heat island effects occur when a proliferation of impervious land cover, that absorbs sunlight rather than reflects it, causes ambient temperature to rise. The increased heat and poor air quality exacerbates pre-existing health conditions of those living in poverty. In suburban and rural areas, people living in poverty experience catastrophic loss due to wildfires because they are unable to finance precautionary measures that would protect their homes or insure them against potential loss.

Pollution is immediate, local, and sometimes visible to the naked eye. In China and India, hundreds of thousands of people die prematurely each year due to air pollution. A major cause of air pollution is burning of fossil fuels for energy, industrial production, and automobiles. Pollutants contaminate a significant percentage of China's river basins, underground water, and farmland soil. A major cause of water pollution is waste disposal practices associated with industrial production. Even in Europe, air pollution due to emissions from diesel cars and burning of coal kills hundreds of thousands of people each year. People with high incomes can purchase air purification systems or fresh air ventilation systems for their homes to mitigate the detrimental effects of air pollution. With respect to water pollution, the same is true of water purification and filtration systems. People living in poverty, however, cannot afford these systems.

Concern about the disproportionate impacts of pollution on those living in poverty raise the question of whether environmental outcomes are just. Does society intentionally place environmental hazards close to those living in poverty? Alternatively, do those living in poverty gravitate towards areas where environmental hazards are more prevalent because the cost of living there is affordable? The answers to these questions depend on whether cause and effect can be determined. A key issue in this regard is whether the siting of environmental hazards such as pollution-producing factories pre-dates the establishment of nearby communities of people living in poverty. While the topography of a given piece of land is arguably predetermined, it is much less clear whether the social, political, and economic considerations that govern how that land is used captures fully the potential unintended environmental consequences for people living on that land.

The consequences of family structure, health, education, assets, and the environment often manifest themselves in the labour market. We take a closer look at this in Chapter 5.

Chapter 5
Labour markets

Questions and policies

For most people, their performance in the labour market determines their station in life. What determines who earns what in the labour market? Are there systemic impediments that inhibit the ability of particular groups to prosper in the labour market? What is the role of education, skills, race, and gender? Are there ways to make the financial return on work greater regardless of skill level? If skills are lacking, are there policies that directly help to close skill gaps? Confrontation of these questions may connect us more closely with what is at the core of our concerns about newcomers to our labour markets who arrive via immigration.

Poverty is associated with weak or no attachment to the labour market and low earnings. Barriers to strong labour market attachment include low educational attainment, social stratification, and discrimination. Education is of particular importance because it influences both labour market attachment and earnings. Public policies relating to apprenticeships, job training, minimum wages, conditional tax credits, and immigration try to improve on real world outcomes produced by unfettered labour markets.

Unfettered labour markets

An unfettered labour market is one where policymakers let supply
and demand for labour find their own equilibrium. Like a set of
weighing scales, they come to a steady state of balance when they
equal each other. While rarely found in the real world, the allure of
an unfettered labour market remains ever present in the minds of
those who believe that government policymakers should not regulate
the labour market. The idea is that employers could set their wages
to the level at which workers are prepared to accept for employment.

On the supply side of the labour market are people who decide
whether to enter the labour market and, if entered, how many
hours to work per unit of time, say a day, week, month, or year.
Preferences about work and leisure and the market wage govern
the number of hours worked, if any. For some people, the current
market wage will be insufficient to induce them to work. Their
non-waged activities are such that it is not worth it to work
currently. This might be the case for a parent who has decided
to provide care to a young child.

If someone does decide to work, then the question is how many
hours to work each day. The answer depends on the hourly market
wage foregone because of enjoying an hour of leisure. As the wage
rate rises, an hour of leisure becomes more expensive. A person's
preferences may be such that she does not want to incur this loss
of the wage. If so, she will work an additional hour to gain the
market wage. Thus, our initial intuition is that in response to an
increase in the market wage, a person will usually supply more
labour so that there is a positive relationship between the market
wage and labour supply.

The market wage is not the sole determinant of someone's labour
supply, however. Anything that makes someone wealthier might

induce that person to reduce the number of hours supplied per unit of time at any given wage. For example, if someone wins a lottery that results in a significant financial windfall, then that person would most likely work less at any given market wage.

The demand for labour by firms reflects their desire to produce goods and services. For example, when a pencil factory wants to make more pencils, the manager will ask an employee to work an additional hour. Suppose the employee agrees and in that hour, she produces twenty pencils. That increment to output is the marginal product of labour. If asked to work yet another hour in that same day, the employee will produce fewer pencils, say only eighteen more, because she may have already worked a full shift and she is getting tired. If the factory sells the last increment to output, the eighteen pencils, at the market price (say, $2 per pencil), then the firm receives additional revenue ($36): its marginal revenue. Now, we are able to consider how much a firm is willing to pay for an additional hour of labour. That amount is the market value of output produced during that additional hour of labour ($36). The amount that the firm actually has to pay for an additional hour of labour, however, is the market wage. If the market wage is less than the amount the firm is willing to pay for labour, then the firm will hire more labour. As the wage rises, the firm is willing to hire fewer workers. Thus, there is an inverse relationship between the quantity of labour demanded by a firm and the market wage, other things held constant.

The market wage is not the sole determinant of a firm's demand for labour, however. Anything that makes workers more productive or that raises demand for the firm's product will raise the quantity of labour that the firm demands at any wage. If workers become more productive because of education or technological improvement, for example, then firms will demand more labour. If consumer tastes turn in favour of the good produced by the firm or if consumer income rises, for example, then the firm will demand more labour at any wage.

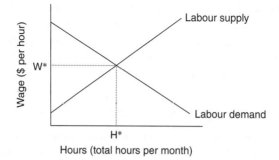

5. Labour market equilibrium.

The interaction of labour demand and supply determines the
wage that people are paid and the amount of employment in
the market. Figure 5 depicts an equilibrium in the labour market
where the lines intersect at wage W* and total hours H*. Suppose
workers become more productive. This would cause the labour
demand line to shift to the right. Firms would be willing to pay
a higher wage at any given level of employment. The equilibrium
wage and equilibrium level of employment would rise. Alternatively,
consider what would happen if workers became wealthier. In this
case, they would supply less labour at every wage. The labour
supply line would shift leftward. This would cause the equilibrium
wage to rise and the equilibrium level of employment to fall.

Because of the labour market's importance in the everyday lives
of people, policymakers ask their labour market analysts very
specific questions about it. First, if the hourly wage is increased,
how will the number of hours that people are willing to work
change? Using data, analysts estimate the percentage change in
hours supplied in response to a 1 per cent change in the market
wage. Second, how much will businesses reduce their demand
for hours of labour in response to an increase in the wage?
Analysts also estimate the percentage change in hours demanded
in response to a 1 per cent change in the market wage. Intuitively,
these responses are analogous to the tautness or slackness of a

rubber band. A taut rubber band does not respond very much, if at all, to a small pull. A slack rubber band responds a lot to a small pull. Analogously, analysts' estimates give policymakers guidance about how employment is likely to respond to policies that 'pull' the market wage in one direction or another.

Minimum wages and living wages

In an effort to support the earnings of low-skilled workers, more than one hundred countries worldwide impose compulsory wage floors in the form of a minimum wage. A minimum wage set below the equilibrium wage will not have any impact on wages or employment. A motivation for setting a minimum wage that is higher than the equilibrium wage for low-skilled workers is that the equilibrium wage is unable to raise someone working full-time year-round out of poverty.

The introduction of a minimum wage raises the price of labour. The focus on employment effects resulting from the introduction of or increase in the minimum wage is justified by concern for earnings of low-skilled workers. Monthly earnings are the product of the hourly wage and the number of hours worked during the month at that wage. If the minimum wage is slightly higher than the equilibrium wage, then its potential distortion of market equilibrium will be small. Thus, it is likely to cause little or no employment loss and some small gain in wages for low-skilled workers. If the minimum wage is set much higher than the equilibrium wage for low-skilled workers, then it may affect the level of employment. Whether it does or not depends on factors such as the size of the deviation from the equilibrium wage, the response of labour demand to a wage change, the number of workers covered by the law, and the degree of compliance with the law. The most important of these factors is the response of labour demand to a wage change. Minimum wage laws could be a part of a policymaker's anti-poverty tool kit if they lift the wages of low-skilled workers while not reducing hours worked substantially.

In the developing country context, the response of labour demand to a change in the wage is difficult to ascertain. In many developing countries, people work in formal and informal labour markets. The minimum wage may not cover a large percentage of workers in informal occupations. Additionally, low-skilled workers flow between covered and uncovered sectors. Employment levels in uncovered sectors are difficult to track due to their informality. Therefore, when the minimum wage in the covered sector changes, it is difficult to know what really happens to employment. In the case of an increase in the minimum wage, displaced workers in the covered sector may or may not re-emerge in the uncovered sector. Another factor that comes into play in the developing country context is compliance with minimum wage laws. For example, Haroon Bhorat and his collaborators estimate that the non-compliance rate, defined as the percentage of workers who earn below the minimum wage that applies to them, is greater than 50 per cent in sub-Saharan Africa. If employers ignore the minimum wage law and enforcement of compliance is weak, then changes in the minimum wage will have little impact on employment.

In the developed country context, an increase in the minimum wage mainly affects employment and earnings of low-skilled workers and young workers aged 16–24 years old. Therefore, research on the employment effects of minimum wage increases focuses on these demographic groups. In the United States, estimates indicate that a 1 per cent increase in the minimum wage reduces demand for low-skilled workers and young workers by between 0 per cent and 0.2 per cent. European Commission researchers estimate that a 1 per cent increase in the minimum wage also reduces demand for low-skilled workers and young workers between 0 per cent and 0.2 per cent in the EU. These findings are consistent with the view that employment losses associated with small increases in the minimum wage are negligible.

Evidence from the United States, however, indicates that an increase in the minimum wage reduces the poverty rate. The economist Arindrajit Dube estimates that a 1 per cent increase in the minimum wage reduces the poverty rate by between 0.22 per cent and 0.55 per cent. This range of estimates is useful for policy analysis. For example, consider the midpoint of this range, –0.38 per cent. Then, a 10 per cent increase in the minimum wage would reduce the poverty rate by 3.8 per cent, other things held constant.

The poverty-reducing potential of moderate increases notwithstanding, some critics of the minimum wage argue that it does not go far enough. Advocates for the living wage in the United States and the United Kingdom seek to establish a wage floor that covers basic expenses associated with multiple dimensions of well-being. These include expenses such as food, clothing, utilities, healthcare, childcare, transportation, housing, taxes, personal and household goods and services, and social and cultural activities. The viewpoint here is that it is in employers' self-interest to pay their staff well enough for each employee to feel included in society. Employees reciprocate via greater attachment, loyalty, and productivity to the employer.

The living wage can be substantially above the minimum wage. In the United States, the nationwide federal minimum wage was $7.25 per hour in 2017. In response to popular campaigns by living wage advocates, California and New York, two large states with a combined population of sixty million, passed legislation in 2016 to raise their minimum wages in steps to $15 per hour by 2022. In the United Kingdom, the nationwide (excluding London) minimum wage was £7.50 per hour in 2017. The UK government refers to this minimum wage as the living wage. The NGO Living Wage Foundation, however, estimated that the real living wage for the UK (excluding London) was £8.45 per hour in 2017.

Conditional tax credits, redux

If boosting earnings is a direct way to lift individuals and families out of poverty, then it could be reasonable for society to design tax policies that increase the return to working for those living in poverty. One such policy is a conditional tax credit. An example from the United States is the EITC that we discussed in Chapter 3. The EITC increases the return to working by providing a credit against taxes owed that the government pays in cash to the worker if the credit is greater than the amount of taxes owed. It is available only to individuals who work. That is the source of the conditionality. The structure of the EITC is that it has a phase-in range of earnings during which the credit increases with earnings. Next, there is a stationary range during which the credit is constant as earnings increase. Finally, there is a phase-out range during which the credit declines as earnings increase. The thresholds for the three ranges are such that the EITC is only relevant for individuals and families with low to moderate annual earnings. The EITC provides strong incentives for single parents to enter the labour force. The evidence, drawn from analyses of labour supply behaviour following expansions of the credit, indicates that it has been successful at doing this. The employment rate of single mothers, for example, rises after EITC expansions.

Training

A way to make workers more productive is to increase their skills through training. If there is a mismatch between skills of workers and skills required to do certain jobs, then training offers a potential remedy. Some examples of training programmes in developed and developing country contexts follow. They all seek to increase firms' demand for labour.

In the United States, the Adult and Dislocated Worker Program provides training services to unemployed adults with a priority given to those living in poverty. The training is in basic workplace skills (communication and basic computation, for example) and occupational skills. The programme connects workers with potential employers at the community level. The goals of the programme include entry into employment, increased retention once employed, and increased earnings.

In Germany, there is a tradition of apprenticeship, particularly in industry. In an apprenticeship, workers intentionally forego formal liberal education in order to develop specialized knowledge in well-defined occupations for which there is a need for workers. The apprenticeship model strengthens demand for labour because firms know the skills and abilities of workers who have completed apprenticeships. Apprenticeships also weaken the tight relationship between educational attainment, employment, and earnings. In this approach, workers develop skills independent of attainment of advanced academic degrees.

In India, the National Skill Development Corporation (NSDC), a not-for-profit company that is a public–private partnership, provides training for jobs. The motivation for the NSDC is to help close the gap between current skills of the typical worker and skills required by employers in a rapidly developing economy. Workers can receive direct training for jobs in several sectors of the economy including electronics, textiles, chemicals and pharmaceuticals, building and construction, food processing, building hardware and home furnishings, information technology, tourism, hospitality and travel, transportation, warehousing and packaging, entertainment, broadcasting, healthcare, banking, insurance, and finance, and education. The goal of the NSDC is to make workers more attractive to employers by giving them skills the employer can use right away.

In sub-Saharan Africa, the two dominant modes of training are apprenticeships and vocational schools. In an apprenticeship, an individual works directly with a master artisan in a small firm to learn a particular skill such as tailoring or carpentry. During the apprenticeship, the apprentice receives reduced compensation. Once the apprentice acquires the skill, she can start her own business. Apprenticeships lead predominantly to self-employment. Vocational schools curriculums teach specific skills such as how to be a mechanic, mason, or engineer. Graduates from these schools predominantly enter the formal sector and earn wages.

Unemployment and underemployment

A shortcoming of the orthodox model of the labour market is that it does not permit unemployment in equilibrium. When supply of labour equals demand for labour, everyone willing to work at the market wage is working. In reality, however, there is unemployment. That is, there are people who are willing to work at the market wage but they cannot find a job. The labour force is the number of people working plus those who are unemployed. To be unemployed, a person must not be working and be actively searching for a job. The omission of unemployment from the orthodox model is consequential because an incidence of unemployment can initiate a spell of poverty for households who do not have robust financial reserves. From a macroeconomic perspective, a rise in the unemployment rate is associated with an increase in the economy-wide poverty rate.

Unemployment can occur because of structural factors that restrict particular demographic groups from high-quality or even adequate housing, education, and healthcare. Often, societies provide these dimensions of well-being based on a particular geography. Rarely is this geography accidental, as we saw with race-based housing policies in the United States and South Africa in Chapter 1 and Chapter 2. Rather, a social calculus stratifies society across lines of class, race, ethnicity, or socio-economic status. Government supports this geography by law enforcement, a judicial system, and a penal code that not only sustains circumscribed areas, but also ensures that people within them who society penalizes for violations are marked so that the possibility of transformation is difficult even if the individual moves away. How so? Once convicted, the ex-offender may find it difficult to gain employment or to participate in the civic life of the community via voting. In this way, place of origin becomes a barometer of opportunity and potential outcome. Restricted opportunities lead to a higher probability of living in poverty and social exclusion.

It is also possible that a person's attachment to the labour force is weak. Someone can be underemployed. Underemployment occurs when someone only works part-time (thirty-four hours a week or less in the US) because she cannot find full-time work, thirty-five hours or more per week. In the United States, the so-called 'working poor' are people who spend at least twenty-seven weeks per year in the labour force but whose incomes still fall below the official poverty level. Part-time workers are more than three times as likely as full-time workers to be classified as working poor. In Britain, people in working-poor households make up the majority of those living in poverty. A challenge these households face is the unavailability of full-time work. Often, an underemployed worker holds multiple part-time jobs in an attempt to cobble together enough income to make ends meet.

Employment and earnings

The types of jobs created in the labour market and the skills of workers in the labour force determine who is employed and at what wage. High-, medium-, and low-skill jobs exist in the economy. Typically, high-skill jobs such as technicians and managers pay more than low-skill jobs such as food preparation and janitorial services. Earnings are the product of the hourly wage and the number of hours worked per unit of time, say a week, month, or year. People who have high skill levels and work in high-skill jobs have high earnings and are unlikely to experience poverty.

Conversely, people who have low skill levels and work in low-skill jobs have low earnings and are more likely to experience poverty.

In recent decades, labour markets in the United States and in Europe produce jobs that are at these two extremes at the expense of medium-skill jobs (manufacturing, say). A downside of this phenomenon is that there may be increased competition for low-skilled jobs as people with moderate skills who used to work in medium-skill jobs compete with low-skill workers for low-skill jobs. This competition puts downward pressure on earnings at the lower end of the earnings distribution. Since earnings from work constitute a major portion of income for low-income households, low earnings increase the risk of living in poverty.

In the developing country context, employment and earnings are also central to determining whether a household is at risk of living in poverty. In this context, the agricultural sector is highly relevant. For example, in sub-Saharan Africa, South East Asia, and South Asia over 45 per cent of the labour force works in the agricultural sector defined as including agriculture, hunting, fishing, and forestry. With respect to agriculture itself, the size of landholdings varies from very small plots of land used for subsistence farming by a single family to very large farms (greater than 500 hectares) that produce for regional and international markets and that employ several people. Smaller farms are more likely to deploy traditional production methods. These include the use of human and animal labour. Larger farms are more likely to use modern production methods. These include the use of machines and chemicals. Larger farms are also more likely to employ wage labour and the labour force is more likely to be permanent as opposed to temporary.

According to the International Labour Organization, the earnings of agricultural workers are, on average, only about 60 per cent of those working in manufacturing. This earnings gap is due in large part to the fact that worker productivity in the agricultural sector is low. Productivity is low in agriculture because workers in that sector are not as well educated on average as those working in manufacturing and they have less financial and physical capital with which to work. In addition, they must often allocate their time to other kinds of informal income-generating activities, such as trading and home production, in order to make ends meet. In this sense, these workers work many hours in an attempt to sustain a given level of consumption. If their wages increased, it is likely that they would work fewer hours.

In the developing country context more generally, earnings are highly variable. In the manufacturing and service sectors, employers do not always pay workers on a timely basis. Hours or days of employment are sporadic. In the agricultural sector, drought and disease can cause production to fluctuate. The variability of earnings can cause depletions of limited physical and financial assets that could be used to build wealth, thus making graduation out of poverty more difficult.

Education and skills

Higher educational attainment is associated with a stronger attachment to the labour force. Evidence from the United States indicates that employment levels for high-school dropouts fall more during recessions than they do among college graduates. Further, the unemployment rate of high-school dropouts increases more following interest rate increases than does the unemployment rate of college graduates.

There is also an inverse relationship between educational attainment and poverty status; the higher the level of educational attainment, the lower the poverty rate. In the US, the poverty rate for people with no high-school diploma can be more than four times as high as for people with a bachelor's degree or higher. Schooling is a buffer against poverty because it is an engine of earnings. Similarly, in sub-Saharan Africa, more education is associated with higher earnings.

Schooling, cognitive skills, and experience are important determinants of labour market earnings. All things being equal, a better-educated worker is more productive because, among other things, she is better able to learn new tasks, make appropriate decisions, and identify and correct potential problems. Because educated workers are more productive, firms are willing to pay them more. Higher compensation is a potent incentive to acquire more education. The acquisition of education is not costless, however. From the perspective of the individual, she must invest time and effort in order to acquire an education. Additionally, there may be fees (tuition and books, for example) associated with acquiring education. The time spent becoming educated represents time not spent doing something else. That something else includes the possibility of entering the labour market with a lower level of education but earning income currently. Thus, the individual must weigh the benefits of an additional year of education against the costs of the same when deciding how educated to become. The difference between these benefits and costs is the net private rate of return to an additional year of schooling.

The return to schooling tells us the percentage increase in earnings associated with an additional year of education. In the labour market as a whole, this return will depend on the supply of workers with various levels of education relative to firms' demand for workers to fill jobs that require different skill levels. This heterogeneity on both sides of the market notwithstanding, it is possible to estimate an average rate of return to schooling for a country from nationally representative household surveys. Averaging these country-level estimates across regions provides a summary of the return to education in different parts of the world. In the developing country context, Evan Peet and his collaborators estimate that the return to education is approximately 7.6 per cent. This overall figure masks variation across two dimensions:

region and gender. With respect to region, the variation is from Asia at 4.4 per cent to Africa at 9.2 per cent, with Eastern Europe (6.7 per cent) and Latin America (7.9 per cent) falling in-between. With respect to gender, the average return for women is 8.6 per cent while for men it is 7.1 per cent. These rates of return are not that different from those found in developed countries like the United States (around 10 per cent). In the United States, the average return to schooling for women is higher than that for men even though women receive less pay on average than men do.

Discrimination

Discrimination is unequal treatment of a group or groups of people due to a particular attribute such as gender, race, disability, age, or sexual orientation. When discrimination is present in the labour market, it can impede the ability of members of targeted groups to obtain employment. If employed, it can dampen wages and earnings of members of targeted groups. Limitation of employment opportunities and attenuation of earnings due to discrimination can contribute to the disparate rates of unemployment and poverty across demographic groups observed within a society.

Two types of discrimination have received considerable attention. The first is taste-based discrimination as emphasized by Gary Becker. Some employers may prefer workers from a certain group. Employer preferences may reflect personal prejudice, concern that their customers are prejudiced, or concern that their current employees are prejudiced. In either case, employers may be willing to employ only workers who are members of a certain group or to pay a premium to employ them even though they are no more productive than workers who are members of other groups. The second is statistical discrimination as emphasized by Kenneth Arrow and Edmund Phelps. This can occur when an employer's assessment of the likely performance of a prospective employee depends on the prospective employee's qualifications *and* information that summarizes the performance of members of her group. This information may take the form of descriptive statistics (averages and standard deviations, for example). The complication here is that statistical information used to summarize the group may provide little insight into the actual performance of the prospective employee under consideration.

Detecting discrimination is not easy. One approach to testing for discrimination in a local labour market is to conduct an experiment. Two popular forms of such experiments are an audit study and a correspondence study. In an audit study, actual people serving as testers apply in person for jobs at various employers. These testers have been carefully screened by the experimenters to ensure that they have matching physical characteristics (height and weight, for example), substantively identical qualifications (the experimenters create artificial resumes, references, and personal histories), and differ by only one observable characteristic, say race. The null hypothesis under examination is that all of the testers are treated the same in terms of the likelihood of receiving a job offer or a callback for a second interview. The alternative hypothesis is that the testers are not treated the same. Sociologist Devah Pager and her collaborators conduct audit studies in the United States. Evidence from these studies indicates that there is racial discrimination against African Americans in particular labour markets. Employers hire and callback African Americans at a lower rate than whites with identical qualifications.

A correspondence study is similar to an audit study except that there are no testers. The application process is remote in that researchers just submit resumes in response to published or online postings. In a correspondence study, the resumes themselves convey substantively identical qualifications but also reveal an attribute about the applicant (race, gender, or both) that may trigger a differential response from the employer. An attractive feature of this approach is that researchers can readily apply it in a developing country context where employers use attributes such as caste or religion (identifiable by job applicant's name) as the basis for discrimination.

Economists Alan Blinder and Ronald Oaxaca developed another approach to testing for discrimination that uses data from the labour market as a whole to compare average outcomes for disparate demographic groups. The groups might be blacks and whites or men and women, for example. If there were differences in the average level of education and experience across groups, then we would expect there to be differences in average wages across groups. If these productivity measures fail to explain all of the difference in average pay, however, then other factors may come into play. Among these possible other factors is discrimination. It is possible to calculate the fraction of the wage gap that is due to productivity factors and the fraction that is unexplained. To do this, we use survey data collected from individuals on their wages, education, work experience, occupation, industry, union status, race, and gender. For the unexplained fraction to represent discrimination, however, we must account for all other possible reasons for differences in average wages. This can be difficult to do because some of the factors driving differences in average wages may be unobservable; examples include ability and grit.

Using this approach, evidence from the United States is consistent with the view that there is discrimination against women in the labour market. Economists Francine Blau and Lawrence Kahn estimate that on average, employers pay women about 79 per cent of what men are paid. After adjusting for factors such as education, experience, race, industry of employment, and occupation, this percentage rises to about 92 per cent. The adjusted figure is higher because it indicates what a woman's pay would be if her employer compensated for her education, experience, and occupation as if she were a man. There is, however, still an unexplained pay gap of 8 per cent even after making these adjustments.

Immigration

Immigration is the act of moving away from one's native country to a country where one is not a native. There is some controversy over whether immigration is a good thing when it comes to poverty. Whether immigration is a good thing or not depends on whether immigrant workers compete with native workers or are complementary to native workers.

On the one hand, immigration may cause displacement of native workers. Immigrant workers compete with native workers when their skills closely match those of native workers. In this case, immigrant workers can serve as substitutes for native workers. For example, suppose an influx of low-skilled immigrants increases the supply of low-skilled workers. Holding the demand for labour constant, the increase in workers causes wages to fall. Low-income native workers who compete with immigrants for jobs are likely to experience a decline in pay and firms will employ fewer of them. This scenario could engender anxiety about immigration. This anxiety can lead to discrimination against immigrants due to the perception that jobs are scarce. As mentioned in Chapter 1, concern that something valuable is scare is often a basis for discrimination.

On the other hand, immigration reallocates resources (labour in particular) to their most productive use. It also disseminates information about technology and the latest production methods. If skill sets of immigrant workers complement native workers, then firms will expand employment of native workers because of immigration. For example, suppose that immigrant workers are highly skilled and possess entrepreneurial talent. They may start new businesses that employ many native low-skilled workers. In this case, an influx of immigrant entrepreneurs increases demand for low-skilled native workers. Holding the supply of low-skilled native workers constant, the increase in demand will cause wages of low-skilled native workers to rise and firms will employ more of them.

In reality, both high-skill and low-skill people immigrate. On balance, the positive effects of immigration outweigh its negative effects. The adverse effects of immigration can be concentrated on local or regional labour forces. In contrast, the beneficial effects of immigrant labour are diffuse as markets spread benefits thinly across a potentially large number of people who constitute a nationwide consumer base. Consumers benefit from lower prices for goods and services produced by these workers. Firms who employ workers from the expanded labour pool are also more profitable. On net, the weight of evidence from the United States suggests that immigration has a small positive effect on the labour market.

In the United States, economists Brian Duncan and Stephen Trejo estimate that the employment rate of immigrant men with less than twelve years of education (> 90 per cent) is higher than those of native men with the same level of education (approximately 72 per cent). Wages of adult immigrant men in the US are more comparable to native men the longer immigrant men have been in the country and the better is their English proficiency. This finding suggests that a process of assimilation takes place.

In the European context, the evidence suggests that immigrants from non-European countries are less likely to obtain employment in jobs commensurate with their skill level. Relative to natives, they also have a higher probability of being in the lowest decile of the earnings distribution and more likely to be living in poverty.

A goal of labour market policy is to create pathways out of poverty. Well-functioning labour markets facilitate economic mobility of people over the course of their lifetimes and across generations.

Chapter 6
Distribution and mobility

Fluidity and rigidity

We all start out in a given position in society and with a level
of income (or wealth). What determines where we will end up?
Will we be better off than our parents were? For people living
in poverty, the ease or difficulty with which one is able to move
across the income distribution of society is the difference between
hope and despair. Whether this movement is easy or difficult tells
us a lot about a society. If movement is easy, we might think of
society as being fluid; a dynamic place to live and raise a family.
If movement is difficult, we might think of society as being rigid;
not the best place to live and raise a family. We measure this
movement in quintiles of the income distribution. Thus, it is also
helpful to consider the distribution of income.

The distribution of income (or wealth)

An income distribution tells us the percentage of the population
that earns an annual income of a given amount at a particular
point in time. The income distribution for a nation is
straightforward to construct. We begin by ordering the range
of income from its smallest value to its largest value. Next, we
split the range of income into non-overlapping classes. Then, we

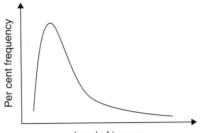

6. Distribution of income.

ask, how many incomes (one per person) fall into each class? Since we know the total population, the per cent of the population that falls into each class is simply the number of people in each class divided by the total population (multiplied by one hundred, of course). That is it. The intuition behind an income distribution is easy to grasp if we visualize drawing a smooth curve over the height of the discrete classes. A simple illustration shows the result of the visualization. Using data from most countries in the world, the income distribution skews to the right as in Figure 6. In Figure 6, the bulk of the population has incomes that are in the lower to middle classes. Beyond the middle classes, fewer people have high incomes. If we had data for the wealth for each member of the population, we could also construct the wealth distribution for each country using the same approach. With wealth replacing income on the horizontal axis, the visualization of the wealth distribution would be just as in Figure 6 except that the figure would skew more to the right.

With the distribution of income in hand, we can ask questions about income inequality, a topic without which a conversation about poverty would be incomplete. Suppose we ordered the population of a country by income. The person with the lowest income would be first in line and the person with the highest income would be last in line. Next, suppose we divided the line

7. Quintiles of the income distribution.

into fifths (quintiles) demarcating each fifth as a bin containing 20 per cent of the population ordered as shown in Figure 7.

If the distribution of income were equal, then each bin would receive 20 per cent of total income. The lowest 40 per cent of the population would receive 40 per cent of total income. That is, the bottom 20 per cent of income earners and the second 20 per cent of income earners constitute the lowest 40 per cent of income earners. Combined, they would receive 40 per cent of total income. The share of total income received by the lowest 40 per cent of income earners is particularly salient because it is a focus of policymakers worldwide, as will be discussed further in Chapter 8.

There is income inequality when each fifth (quintile) of the population does not receive a fifth of total income. According to the World Bank, in no country does the bottom 20 per cent of the population receive more than 11 per cent of total income. Here are some examples of the share of total income received by the bottom fifth in 2015: United States, 5 per cent; France, 8 per cent; India, 8 per cent; Brazil, 3.5 per cent; and Uganda, 6 per cent. For these same countries, here are the shares of total income received by the top fifth: United States, 46 per cent; France, 41 per cent; India, 44 per cent; Brazil, 57 per cent; and Uganda, 49 per cent.

In 1912, the statistician Corrado Gini showed how to use data to calculate a number that represents how unequal is a country's distribution of income. Today, we call that number the Gini coefficient. It varies between zero and one. A value of zero means there is no income inequality. A value of one means that there is extreme income inequality. We shall see examples of Gini coefficients for selected countries when we discuss measurement of intergenerational mobility. Income inequality is not necessarily problematic. It could simply represent differential rewards to skill, innovation, and luck. When it becomes a hindrance to mobility, however, graduation from poverty becomes much more difficult.

Lifetime mobility

Lifetime mobility focuses on the ability of people to change their position in society's income distribution within their lifetime. If it is highly likely that a person will move from one quintile of the income distribution to another over her life course and that this is true for most people, then we would characterize society as highly mobile.

If we are willing to interpret 'getting ahead in life' as a rough proxy for improving one's position in society's income or wealth distributions, then Pew Research Center global surveys are clear as to what people believe are the keys to advancement: having a good education, working hard, knowing the right people, and being lucky. Generally, there is confidence in free markets and the rewards that they dispense. Americans in particular subscribe to individualism. More than 70 per cent of them believe that hard work is very important to getting ahead in life. Americans are also least likely (only 40 per cent) to agree that forces outside of their control determine success in life. Globally, attitudes about individualism and self-determination are more mixed. The global median is that 50 per cent of people believe that hard work is very important to getting ahead in life. In response to a separate question, however, a majority of people in the rest of the world believe that forces outside of their control determine success in life.

Poverty transitions

What can we say about mobility at the lower end of the income distribution? This question brings us to the issue of transitions into and out of poverty. If a large group of households are observed over time, it is likely that some of them that are initially above a given poverty threshold will fall below it while some of them that are initially below the threshold will rise above it. Some households that rise above the threshold will stay above it. Others will fall back below it after some period. Similarly, some households that fall below the threshold will stay below it. Others will rise above it after some period. There can be mobility across the poverty line in both directions within the lifetime of current household members.

The factors that influence spells of poverty do not always conform to popular narratives of mobility. Leading factors associated with entry into poverty include changes in family structure, such as divorce, and a decline in earnings of the head of household due to job loss. Factors associated with exit from poverty include marriage (again, a change in family structure) and a rise in earnings of the head of household.

According to the economist Ann Huff Stevens, what also matters for poverty transitions is how long the household has been living in or out of poverty in the recent past. The longer the household has been living in poverty, the lower the probability that it will exit poverty in the near future. Possible reasons for this relationship include an erosion of labour market skills that can accompany detachment from the labour force. The longer the household has not lived in poverty, the higher the probability that the household will exit a spell of poverty. The intuition here is that from time to time some households living above the poverty line have a bad year due to, say, poor health of a main earner. Once that main earner is back on her feet, then earnings return to normal levels thereby restoring the household's previous living standard. The key notion here is that of duration dependence: the length of a spell of poverty can be useful in determining how likely it is that a household will transition out of poverty. In the United States, for example, the impact of duration varies across demographic characteristics. African Americans, female-headed households, and those with lower than a high-school diploma are less likely than whites are to transition out of poverty for any given length of a current poverty spell.

The household exists within the broader macroeconomy. The performance of the economy as a whole can have an impact on the probability that a household moves across a poverty threshold. During an expansion in economic activity, jobs are easier to find. Significant drivers of poverty exits are the degree of attachment to the labour market of the household head (in the form of weeks worked per year) and the amount of pay at the lower end of the wage distribution. More work and higher pay increase the probability that a household will exit poverty.

Intergenerational mobility

When considering economic mobility across generations, it is useful to distinguish between mobility in an absolute sense versus a relative sense. Absolute mobility answers the question, is a person's income (or wealth) greater than that of her parents at the same age? Relative mobility answers the question, is a person's position or rank in the income (or wealth) distribution higher than that of her parents at the same age? The reason we care about relative mobility is that a person's income could be greater than that of her parents at the same age yet the person could have fallen behind in the sense that many people in society experienced increases in income such that her position (rank) in the income distribution is lower. This would be an example of upward mobility in the absolute sense but not in the relative sense.

Do societies transmit economic status across generations? One perspective on this question emphasizes private considerations, in particular, human capital transmission from parents to their children. An alternative perspective emphasizes structural factors in society that may constrain children to remain in the occupation or social class of their parents. We consider each perspective in turn.

If we assume that parents care how their children will fare in the labour market, then they will invest in their children's education. How much parents invest is constrained by their income and their desire to consume goods and services currently. Given parents' current income, the more they consume, the fewer resources are available for investment in their children's education and vice versa. The economist Gary Solon suggests that the optimal amount of investment in education balances the trade-off between consumption and investment to maximize parents' satisfaction. This optimal amount of investment is increasing in parents' after-tax income, the earnings return (received by their children) on investment in education, and the degree of altruism parents have for their children. Regardless of the amount of educational investment, however, parents pass to their children a certain amount of innate ability that along with the child's education represents the child's stock of human capital. The stock of human capital is, according to this perspective, the main determinant of the child's earnings capacity in the labour market.

Parents' investment decisions and the genetic component of ability establish the intergenerational link between parental income and the income of their children. The higher is parental income, the more they invest in the education of their children. The more educated the children, the higher is their human capital and the higher are their earnings. This perspective does not imply that the degree of pass-through of income from generation to generation is one-for-one. Across generations, the rate of return on investment in education varies. In addition, genetic variation occurs such that it is unlikely that children will have the same level of ability as their parents.

Sociologists such as William Julius Wilson offer an alternative perspective on the question of intergenerational transfer of economic status. They place emphasis on broader considerations such as social capital and neighbourhood effects that influence individuals and families.

Social capital represents the idea that most people are part of a network. The ties that bind the network together are overlapping factors including ethnicity, religious affiliation, race, and profession. The network is a locus of trust and support for each person in it. An important issue, however, is the network's capacity to help people in it get certain things done. If the network gives someone access to productive opportunities and outcomes (a higher-paying job, for example) that she would not have access to otherwise, then the network has a high degree of social capital. These connections between people reflect the structure of social relations and institutions in society as a whole. People are constrained by their social capital to a particular neighbourhood, occupation, or class. These constraints inhibit their ability to accumulate the amount of human capital they desire, to live in communities of their choosing, and even to maintain a level of health that facilitates overall well-being. There is limited scope for self-selection or self-determination. If their children grow up in similar circumstances, then they will receive from their parents an attenuated amount of social and human capital that is likely to impair their life chances by reducing their economic and social opportunities. Family background and position within the broader structure of social relations itself thus becomes a determinant of future prospects. Of course, a newborn child has no control over this precondition. For those living in poverty, this dynamic process is a mechanism for intergenerational transfer of poverty status.

Neighbourhood effects are possible negative or positive spillovers associated with place that affect households. Neighbourhoods are geographical units consisting of certain institutions, social norms, and people. The relevant institutions include schools, places of worship, community centres, health facilities, and libraries. Social norms include levels of civic participation, educational attainment, military service, volunteerism, and philanthropy. Locations with high levels of civic participation, good schools, and easy access to high-quality healthcare are likely to imbue residents with advantages over and above those derived within the household. Peer interactions that multiply and deepen individual skills or aptitudes ground these advantages. Along with the people who enliven them, these social norms and institutions form an ecosystem. Exposure to that ecosystem can influence the mobility of individuals and households both within a lifetime and across generations.

The economist Raj Chetty and his collaborators document that extended exposure to a low-poverty neighbourhood provides a leg up in life. Children from low-income households who grow up in a low-poverty neighbourhood earn more as adults than children who are like them apart from the fact that the latter grew up in a neighbourhood with a high poverty rate. They are also more likely to attend college. Girls are less likely to give birth as teenagers. Boys benefit especially from growing up in areas with low crime rates. Boys from low-income households who grow up in low-crime areas earn more as adults than their counterparts do who grew up in areas with higher crime rates. The positive effects of growing up in low-poverty neighbourhoods spill over to subsequent generations. Higher educational attainment improves the economic opportunities available to children from low-income households as adults. The higher earnings associated with more education permit them to live in better neighbourhoods. Thereby, the next generation of children receive the benefit of living in a low-poverty neighbourhood.

Measure of intergenerational mobility

To measure the degree of intergenerational mobility, we calculate the percentage change in a child's income at a given age relative to a 1 per cent change in income of the child's parent at that same age. To calculate this measure, income data for children and parents when they were approximately the same age are required. For example, the comparison would be between, say, the earnings of a person aged 40 with that of her parent at age 40. It is useful to calculate this measure when possible. For example, if this measure equals zero, then it indicates that there is no relationship between changes in parental and child income when they were both the same age. In this case, the fact that the parent's status improved at a given age tells us nothing about what is likely to happen to the child's status at that same age. Such a finding would be consistent with a society where there is a high degree of mobility across percentiles of the income distribution. In contrast, if this measure equals one, then it indicates that there is a one-to-one relationship between changes in parental and child income when they both were the same age. In this case, a decline in parent's status at a given age is associated with a parallel decline in the child's status at that same age. Such a finding would be consistent with a society where there is a low degree of mobility (really, none) across percentiles of the income distribution between generations.

The economist Miles Corak reports intergenerational earnings mobility for fathers and their sons (aged 20–45) in a cross-section of countries. In Table 10, we pair those data with Gini coefficients from a select set of countries to illustrate his general finding. When we look across countries, there is a positive relationship between initial inequality and subsequent rigidity. Put differently,

Table 10 Income inequality and intergenerational mobility

Country	Gini coefficient (in 1985)	Intergenerational earnings mobility (post-1985)
Brazil	0.59	0.58
United States	0.42	0.47
Pakistan	0.32	0.46
Finland	0.22	0.18

N.B. Intergenerational earnings mobility is the percentage change in a child's income at a given age relative to a 1 per cent change in income of the child's parent at that same age. The Gini coefficients are from the World Bank's All the Ginis database.

more income inequality is associated with less intergenerational income mobility. There is no simple story that explains this association because countries have different histories, cultures, and political systems. In Chapter 7, however, we consider possible reasons for this association based on the ability of prosperous groups to perpetuate their status.

Poverty traps

Is it possible for an entire country to be 'stuck' at such a low level of income per capita that it cannot escape poverty? What about subgroups within a particular country? Can we relegate these subgroups to living in poverty amid general prosperity? The answer to these questions is 'yes', under certain conditions. Imagine trying to roll a ball up a hill. If the amount of energy applied to rolling the ball is not great enough, then the ball will roll back down the hill. Small amounts of energy applied to the task will not get it done. What is required is a critical level of energy, an amount sufficient to traverse the summit of the hill. A poverty trap represents something parallel to this hypothetical situation. In a poverty trap, small incremental improvements are undone by countervailing forces that cause society or subgroups to relapse into a prior state of deprivation. Conditions that can lead to poverty traps include the presence of critical thresholds, dysfunctional institutions, and membership effects.

Poverty can trap a society when small improvements in average wealth or education are not enough to graduate society to a higher steady-state level of income per capita or well-being. Small improvements may not provide the buffer needed to absorb shocks (poor health, bad weather, and diseased livestock, for example) that may hit the typical low-income household. Average wealth has to be high enough so that transitory setbacks do not lead to sustained dissipations of wealth.

If society draws the most talented entrepreneurs into corrupt or violent enterprises rather than legitimate production for the market economy, then overall output of the economy will be lower than it would be otherwise. Small surges in legitimate productive activity only increase the harvest for the corrupt. Eventually, entrepreneurs withdraw from the legal economy, deciding to do nothing, or worse, perhaps resurfacing on the illegitimate side of the economy. The problem here is the absence (or dysfunction) of institutions (rule of law and property rights enforcement, for example) required to support an equilibrium where the level of legal entrepreneurship is high.

To the extent that a person identifies herself with a particular group or set of groups, perceptions of that group may influence her in certain circumstances. For example, suppose a teacher heightens a student's awareness of group identity just before taking a test. A phenomenon that social psychologists Claude Steele and Joshua Aronson label stereotype threat is the finding that the student may perform worse than expected on the test. For reasons far beyond a person's control, negative spillovers may accrue to groups with which the person is associated. These negative spillovers can affect the return on personal investments that the person might undertake. If the return on personal investments is artificially low, then the person could rationally respond by reducing the amount of investment in the productive activity. Because of lower investment, the accumulated level of productive capacity will be lower in the future than it would otherwise have been. If this lower level is insufficient to lift the person out of poverty, then poverty will persist.

The key here is the presence of negative spillovers pinned on group affiliation. A person may have little control over the group with which society identifies her. Yet, the affiliation can affect her private rate of return on investment. If the affiliation lowers her rate of return, then suboptimal (relative to the no spillover situation) levels of investment may occur. This is an example of how group membership can trap subgroups of people in persistent poverty.

A policy implication that follows from thinking about poverty traps is that in some circumstances interventions that move an entire society or an entire subgroup to a position that is significantly different from their original position may be necessary to break a cycle of poverty.

Immigration and emigration

Immigration and emigration are acts of movement. The World Bank tracks these movements of people and their remittances. Remittances are the monies that movers send to those they leave behind. Remittances are an anti-poverty lifeline. They represent a source of income that compensates, at least partially, for the physical absence of a productive member of the household.

Each year, hundreds of millions of people worldwide leave their native countries in search of upward economic mobility for themselves and their children. Where they end up depends in part on where they start. More than three-quarters of migrants from Latin America and the Caribbean immigrate to an OECD country. About half of migrants from the Europe and Central Asia region and the Latin America and Caribbean region immigrate to an OECD country. The other half of migrants from these regions immigrate to other countries within the regions themselves. Less than two-fifths of migrants from the Middle East and North Africa region, South Asia, and sub-Saharan Africa immigrate to an OECD country. In the Middle East, a majority of the reminder of emigrants immigrate to other countries within the region. South Asia emigrants are attracted to oil-rich countries in the Persian Gulf region. Most migrants from sub-Saharan Africa immigrate to other countries within the region.

Evidence from the United States suggests that immigration fosters economic mobility. Brian Duncan and Stephen Trejo show that once we take education into account, wage gaps between workers from families who have been in the country for three or more generations and first-generation immigrants are large and statistically significant. On the other hand, wage gaps between workers from families who have been in the country for three or more generations and workers from families who have been in the country for two generations are small and statistically insignificant. This suggests that over time there is some convergence in labour market outcomes across generations.

Economic mobility is an antidote to poverty. Movers seek improved lives for themselves and their families. Whether their lives improve depends in part on the policies that society adopts to combat poverty.

Chapter 7
Combating poverty

Helpful knowledge

Although poverty reduction has not occurred as fast as anyone would like, we know a considerable amount about what is helpful in the struggle against poverty. Perhaps just as important, we know a lot about what is not helpful. What seems to reduce poverty? What does not? Moreover, how do we know?

Role of economic growth and inequality

The World Bank classifies countries into one of four income groups based on income per capita: low, lower-middle, upper-middle, and high. Before 1997, China was a member of the low-income country group. In 1997, China transitioned from the low-income group to the lower-middle income group. Just thirteen years later, in 2010, China jumped from the lower-middle income group to the upper-middle income group. In 1981, China's poverty rate was 88.3 per cent based on the headcount ratio at $1.90 a day (2011 PPP$). In 2010, this poverty rate was 11.2 per cent. This remarkable accomplishment was due in large part to rapid economic growth over this period. Thirty years of economic growth lifted over 700 million people out of extreme poverty in China.

A source of China's rapid growth over this thirty-year period was economic reforms introduced in the late 1970s. The economist Martin Ravallion documents that these reforms included reallocation of collectivized land to individual farmers, relaxation of the requirement that the government could buy a portion of farm output at discount prices, and adoption of policies that enhanced absorption of labour into the expanding manufacturing sector as the agricultural sector released it. Importantly, China began its reform period with relatively mild income, educational, and asset inequality. Thus, as growth accelerated, its benefits were widely dispersed across the population.

The official headcount poverty rate in the United States in 1959 was 22.4 per cent. In 1973, this measure of poverty hit its all-time low of 11.1 per cent. Despite two minor recessions during this period, the average annual real gross domestic product (GDP) per capita growth rate in the US was 3.1 per cent. This robust growth rate was an important driver in reducing the poverty rate. From 1959 to 1973, economic growth lifted over sixteen million Americans out of poverty. Yet, here too there was an important initial condition. In 1959, the share of the top decile families in US national income was approximately 33 per cent. With the benefit of hindsight, we know that this entire period was one of relatively mild income inequality. Thus, as growth accelerated, its benefits were widely dispersed across the population.

These historical episodes in China and the United States suggest that economic growth can drive poverty reduction in the context of developing and high-income countries. Whether growth alone is sufficient for poverty reduction is debatable. As noted in the examples of China and the US, a particular initial condition, that of relatively mild income inequality, accompanied rapid economic growth. Given there will always be some income inequality, the key appears to be that it is mild so that it does not mitigate the poverty-reducing effects of growth. How might this occur? Some inequality may be desirable as a reward for invention, innovation, and risk taking that catalyses growth.

If there is severe inequality, however, the affluent may be able to use their position in society to ensure that a disproportionate share of the proceeds from growth accrues to them. For example, the affluent may use their wealth to keep power in the hands of individuals or parties that share their political ideology or to keep their taxes lower than would otherwise be the case. Such actions could curtail the size of the public sector and thereby restrict broad access to the best schools and healthcare thereby ensuring that society preserves social positions across generations. In Chapter 2, we saw a historical episode where severe inequality prevented European colonies from growing rapidly as the Industrial Revolution took off in Western Europe. European elites in the colonies were able to use their wealth and power to implement policies that thwarted any broad-based sharing of prosperity.

Role of governance and institutions

Governance is the exercise of authority. In democratic societies, the governed grant the authority to govern to a subset of the citizenry. The electoral process is consequential in a representative democracy because it determines which institutions prevail. Legislative processes and election outcomes also determine how the state deploys its assets. Importantly, representative democracies that give people a choice between two or more viable alternatives are more likely to settle on inclusive institutions that promote broad-based economic growth. In more autocratic societies, constraints on the executive branch are limited. Political, economic, social, regulatory, and allocative power are concentrated in the hands of a few. The few are more likely to use state assets to perpetuate their position. A vital mechanism for doing this is the adoption of extractive institutions.

Corruption is the abuse of public position for private gain. In effect, it is a tax on creativity, initiative, and entrepreneurship. It undermines trust that is the foundation of contracts and markets. When the state is corrupt, people have few means for redressing wrongs perpetrated against them. In this case, systemic corruption is a mechanism by which the state extracts resources from people. The evidence suggests that in some slow-growing high-poverty areas of the world, corruption is pervasive.

According to a Transparency International survey in 2015, one in five sub-Saharan Africans pays at least one bribe because of coming into contact with a public service official. The points of contact with the state for which bribes are paid include public schools, public healthcare, public utilities (water and electricity provision, for example), document and permit procurement, the courts, and the police. The highest rate of bribe-paying occurs in contact with courts and the police. This finding supports the view that ability to pay is central to whether authorities respect certain basic rights. A few countries in sub-Saharan Africa have made relative progress against corruption. These include Botswana, Lesotho, Burkina Faso, and Senegal.

For developing countries, violence in the form of civil or international wars inhibits a society's ability to reduce poverty. In fact, it is likely to make poverty worse. Infrastructure (roads, bridges, facilities, power stations, and ports) is the backbone of private sector economic activity and provision of public services, such as education and healthcare. Warfare lays waste to the land and infrastructure; it also destroys the most vital asset of any society, the people themselves. Rates of infant mortality and malnourishment rise because of warfare. Life expectancy necessarily declines among the civilian and military population. Society cannot easily replace the lost talents and human capital of highly creative or entrepreneurial people. Add to these costs those associated with the use of public funds to raise, maintain, and arm the military.

Even in high-income countries, poverty reduction is more difficult in the presence of warfare. President Lyndon Johnson launched the Great Society in the United States in 1964. That introduced a number of social programmes designed to reduce poverty in America. These programmes included Medicare, Medicaid, Food Stamps (now Supplemental Nutrition Assistance), and Job Corps. As discussed further in Chapter 8, the goal of these programmes was to eradicate poverty and to create a robust social safety net that would provide support to those who were not full participants in the economic growth of the 1960s. America's participation in the Vietnam War compromised the war on poverty. The US government diverted precious domestic resources (fiscal, personnel, and strategic) into the Vietnam War effort. Few people would argue that the poverty rate of 11.1 per cent reached in 1973 was sufficient to claim victory over poverty. By the mid-1970s, poverty reduction was no longer prominent on the national policy agenda.

Institutions are rules that people live by. Some institutions contribute to poverty reduction. Some do not. Economists Daron Acemoglu and James Robinson introduce a useful classification of institutions: inclusive and extractive institutions. Inclusive institutions encourage broad-based participation in the economic and political life of a society. They enhance economic growth by proving individuals with incentives to work, save, invest, innovate, and to take risks. They allow individuals to retain a significant share of rewards from their efforts. Examples of inclusive institutions include equal protection under the law and secure property rights. Extractive institutions channel the benefits of a society's economic activity into the hands of only a narrow segment of society. They stifle economic growth by reducing the return to individual initiative and creativity. Examples of extractive institutions include a prohibition on private property, state-sponsored coercion, and of course the extreme, slavery.

Table 11 summarizes the relationship between governance, institutions, and poverty. The upper left cell containing inclusive

Table 11 Institutions and societal outcomes

	Inclusive political	**Extractive political**
Inclusive economic	Growth and prosperity	Instability
Extractive economic	Instability	Stagnation and poverty

economic and political institutions is consistent with sustained poverty reduction. The cells on the counter-diagonal, from top right to bottom left, produce instability eventually. Inclusive political institutions give rise to greater voice by those exploited under an extractive economic regime leading to political reform. Inclusive economic institutions give rise to a broad middle class under an extractive political regime leading to the desire for greater political say. The transitions implied by these periods of instability need not be smooth. In both cases, emergent people displace entrenched interests. The likelihood of collateral damage is high. Extractive political and economic institutions yield economic stagnation and poverty.

How does the institutional approach fare in practice? Acemoglu and Robinson offer examples of countries that fit into each cell. South Korea and China have experienced periods of rapid economic growth and poverty reduction. Thus, the first row of Table 12 suggests that economic growth can occur under different political systems. China's lack of political pluralism is a source of its underlying instability. It is unclear what would happen in China if its expanding middle class began to press for greater political representation. Somalia and North Korea are low-income countries that have been that way for a long time. The second row of Table 12 suggests that stagnation can occur under different political systems. In Somalia, the rule of law cannot take hold because political power is too decentralized. Incessant competition for political power is a source of its instability. A market economy cannot develop and flourish under these conditions.

Table 12 Institutions across countries

	Inclusive political	Extractive political
Inclusive economic	South Korea	China
Extractive economic	Somalia	North Korea

Markets and trade

As Adam Smith articulated in *The Wealth of Nations*, markets permit individuals to specialize in productive activities by providing many opportunities to trade with others. Specialization enhances productivity by fostering learning-by-doing and innovation. Markets also provide vital information about resource allocation. Market prices are signposts that indicate which resources are plentiful or scarce relative to demand for them. Market participants read these signposts and make decisions about how to deploy their talents and assets. When the price of a good is high, firms are encouraged to produce more of that good and consumers are encouraged to purchase less of that good. Conversely, when the price for a good is low, firms are encouraged to produce less of that good and consumers are encouraged to purchase more of that good. Because of this interaction between buyers and sellers, the price of the good adjusts up or down and eventually settles at the level observed in the market.

The advantages that accrue to firms and individuals because of participating in markets carry over to nations as well. That is, a nation can specialize in productive activities according to its comparative advantage. Then, by trading with other nations, it can make itself better off. A nation has a comparative advantage in an activity for which its opportunity cost of performing it is lowest among all possible alternatives. Markets lower the risk of specializing according to one's comparative advantage. The reason is that nations will produce more of all goods because of specialization according to comparative advantage. As a result, there are more goods to share among nations. This is not to say that international trade will not hurt some people. It is likely that within any one country, imports of products that compete with domestically produced goods will harm some people. The net benefits of trade, however, outweigh the harm it might do. The evidence suggests that participation in international trade or trade liberalization reduces poverty on average when the nation has good governance, well-educated people, and a well-developed financial sector.

When markets are absent or function poorly, poverty reduction is more difficult. An important example in this regard is the credit market. A poorly functioning credit market could mean that a rural farmer in a developing country may not be able to obtain the financing needed to purchase seed, fertilizer, equipment, and materials required to plant her crops and to tide her household over until harvest. The lack of financing could force the farmer to forego farming and to turn to other activities to which she is not as well suited. Her earnings in these alternate activities are likely to be less than would have been the case otherwise. The dampening of her earnings is likely to make it more difficult for her family to transition out of poverty.

Restricted access to the formal or standard credit market can also hamper people living in poverty in high-income countries. In the United States, for example, households with little savings and impaired credit histories sometimes turn to high-cost, short-term loans to pay bills or buy groceries. The ability to borrow against one's next pay cheque is the defining feature of these so-called 'payday' loans. Customers who have taken out multiple loans over the calendar year hold most of the payday loans outstanding. In addition, it is common for the borrower to renew the loan on the same day that she repays the previous loan. Consequently, there is some risk that these loans could lure borrowers into a revolving door of interest payment and loan renewal that could leave borrowers worse off financially because of increased net indebtedness.

Why are markets absent? Why do markets sometimes function poorly? A prominent answer to both questions is imperfect information: parties entering into a trade do not hold all the information about the situation they are entering.

Moral hazard is a situation where the consummation of a contract creates an incentive for one party to engage in riskier behaviour because the contract insulates the risk-taking party from significant loss in the presence of negative outcomes. A classic example in this regard is insurance. Once someone obtains insurance, the insured person has less incentive to self-insure by being careful. If moral hazard is pervasive, the market for insurance can fail to exist. If the pool of the insured is composed mostly of risk-loving people, then the payouts are likely to exceed premiums paid to the insuring party. This imbalance will eventually cause insurance providers to withdraw from the market.

Adverse selection is a situation where the offer of a contract attracts mainly those who are more likely to require payout from the contract. Again, insurance provision is a useful context for illustration. People who are unhealthy or people who believe that the probability that they will be unhealthy in the future is high are most likely to demand health insurance. If the pool of the insured is composed mostly of unhealthy people, then payouts for healthcare are likely to exceed premiums paid to the insuring party. This imbalance will eventually cause insurance providers to withdraw from the market.

The underlying difficulty in both situations is an asymmetry of information. The insurer does not know who the risk-loving or unhealthy people are. The extension to credit markets is immediate. For credit markets to function properly, participants need to know certain information on a case-by-case basis, the riskiness of the proposed project and the creditworthiness of the borrower, to start. If both parties to the contract cannot agree upon the veracity of these factors, it is unlikely that creditors will extend a loan.

Social safety nets and social protection systems

Because markets sometimes fail, societies often implement social safety nets to support people living in poverty. According to the World Bank, social safety nets 'are noncontributory measures designed to provide regular and predictable support to poor and vulnerable people'. A social safety net can take many forms. In the developing country context, the World Bank focuses on six types of programme: conditional cash transfers, unconditional cash transfers, school feeding programmes, unconditional in-kind transfers, public works, and fee waivers. Conditional cash transfers provide cash payments conditional on the execution of some prescribed action such as presentation of children for regular health check-ups. Unconditional cash transfers provide cash payments at regular intervals without preconditions. School feeding programmes provide meals to children who attend school. Unconditional in-kind programmes provide goods (food and shelter, for example) without preconditions. Public works provide employment in construction of public goods such as roads and schools. Finally, governments provide fee waivers to cover vital expenses for health or education.

An argument for a social safety net is that it sustains members of society who experience a stint of poverty. It enables people to rebound faster from negative shocks, alleviates the pressure to destroy productive assets (such as livestock), and permits people to deploy their talents more readily. Its presence improves peoples' health and well-being. The evidence suggests that this argument is gaining traction in developing counties where most of the people living in poverty worldwide reside. Over eighty low-income and lower-middle-income countries have at least one kind of social safety net programme. While school feeding programmes are the most prevalent, the fastest growing are cash transfer programmes. On average, low-income and lower-middle-income countries spend approximately 1.6 per cent of GDP on social safety net programmes.

Social safety nets are one component of a social protection system. The other components include programmes for social insurance, health, housing, and labour market policies. A key labour market policy is the minimum wage as discussed in Chapter 5. It places a floor on wages for qualifying jobs. Social insurance programmes generally require a contribution from participants usually paid in the form of taxes on income. In return, participants receive payments if income falls due to unemployment or disability. Additionally, social insurance provides income in old age when the capacity to work may be diminished. In the high-income country context, social protection systems can command a non-trivial share of GDP. In OECD countries, for example, public social spending is approximately 22 per cent of GDP on average. The range is large, from France at over 30 per cent to Mexico at less than 15 per cent. Governments do not direct all of this spending at people living in poverty, however. Of public spending that is in the form of cash, governments direct only about 20 per cent of it towards the lowest income quintile on average across the OECD.

Infrastructure

According to the World Bank, investment in rural infrastructure is a proven strategy for reducing poverty in the developing world. Paved roads, for example, expand job opportunities and lower the cost of transporting agricultural goods to distant markets. More generally, a country's infrastructure is its roads, ports, railways, airports, power generation, water supply, sanitation system, and communication/information technology. It is the channels through which local, regional, and global trade and distribution flow. It facilitates delivery of health and educational services. A robust infrastructure contributes to economic growth and poverty reduction. Unfortunately, in some low-income countries investment in infrastructure is deficient and existing infrastructure is in disrepair.

Nowhere are infrastructure needs greater than in the low-income countries of sub-Saharan Africa. Power disruptions are frequent. Sources of these disruptions include droughts, conflicts, and oil price fluctuations. Low-income countries in sub-Saharan Africa have lower paved road density and total road density, measured in kilometres per 100 square kilometres of arable land, than other low-income countries. They also have less telephone (landline) density, less capacity to generate power, and lower electricity, water, and improved sanitation coverage as a percentage of the population. The situation is better with respect to mobile phone density, where usage for payments and banking leap-frogged traditional technologies. These infrastructure deficits make it difficult for businesses to operate efficiently. There is less trade, specialization, and employment. These deficits are a drag on economic growth.

Infrastructure gaps are difficult to close because they require large-scale financing. The economist Amar Bhattacharya and his collaborators estimate that the cost of closing infrastructure gaps in developing countries are in the range of 6 to 8 per cent of GDP. Possible sources of financing include government, private investors, and international entities such as the Multilateral Development Banks (the World Bank, the African Development Bank, the Asian Development Bank, the European Bank for Reconstruction and Development, and the Inter-American Development Bank). Investment in infrastructure is risky business. Risks to repayment due to political instability, poor macroeconomic performance, and environmental degradation confound efforts to raise the required amounts. Exemplars of rapid poverty reduction and economic growth such as South

Korea in the 1960s indicate that an initial emphasis on ratcheting up infrastructure density and development can pay off for generations to come.

Aid

One possible way to help a country to be less impoverished is to give it money. It could then use that money to pay for schools, health clinics, infrastructure, and vaccines that can improve the well-being of a population. In principle, this is the role of aid in the fight against poverty. Three questions arise immediately. What is aid? How much aid is there? Does aid work?

We focus on a specific type of (foreign) aid: official development assistance (ODA). According to the OECD, ODA is grants and loans provided by a state entity for the 'promotion of the economic development and welfare of developing countries as its main objective'. Loans offered at 25 per cent below market interest rates count as ODA. This discount makes the loans 'concessional in character and conveys a grant element'. Therefore, for example, loans for military and anti-terrorism expenditures do not count as ODA.

The target amount of aid provision by members of the OECD's Development Assistance Committee (DAC) is 0.7 per cent of their gross national income. Included in the twenty-nine member nations of the DAC are the United States, United Kingdom, France, Germany, Australia, Japan, and South Korea. Since 1970, the ratio of ODA to gross national income for the DAC countries as a group has hovered between 0.2 per cent and 0.4 per cent. In constant US dollars (using 2014 prices and exchange rates), the amount of ODA provided by the DAC group was $42.6 billion in 1970 and $146.7 billion in 2015.

On average, the smaller (in terms of population size) a developing country, the larger the amount of aid received per capita. For example, India, with a population of approximately 1,300 million (or 1.3 billion) people, receives about $2 in (net) aid per person per year, while Vietnam, with a population of approximately 91 million people, receives about $46 in (net) aid per person per year. You might think that one plausible reason for the difference is that the need in Vietnam is greater. Annual per capita income in the two countries is approximately the same, however: $1,600 in India and $1,900 in Vietnam in 2014. If we compare annual per capita income in these two countries using international dollars (PPP$), we have India at PPP$5,600 and Vietnam at PPP$5,400. Therefore, India and Vietnam are quite similar in this sense. Yet, the smaller country receives much more aid on a per capita basis.

There is not a broad consensus on the poverty-reducing effectiveness of aid. Some feel that there has been too little aid, others that there has been too much. On the one hand, we have economists such as Jeffrey Sachs and the musician Bono (Paul Hewson) who are adherents of the too-little-aid position. Their view is that aid has to surpass a threshold in order for its poverty-reducing impact to be evident. Aid must address every aspect of a community's situation to lift its inhabitants out of poverty. This means that education, health, farming, and infrastructure should be stimulated simultaneously. The policy prescription is to shower a community with aid in order to block all channels of poverty transmission at once, so that prosperity can take hold and become sustainable. In response to this perspective, we see aid flowing to entire villages in Ethiopia, Kenya, Ghana, Mali, Malawi, Nigeria, Rwanda, Senegal, Tanzania, and Uganda.

On the other hand, we have economists such as William Easterly and Dambisa Moyo who are adherents to the too-much-aid position. Their view is that aid props up bad governments that fail to use the money to promote poverty reduction. Government corruption prevents aid from reaching impoverished citizens. Rather, foreign aid enriches government officials and local elites. It preserves their positions by financing suppression of opposition.

Mobutu Sese Seko's Democratic Republic of the Congo is a classic historical example of this behaviour. Further, according to this view, aid provision is an industry based on the preservation of poverty. Incentives within this industry induce NGOs that implement anti-poverty programmes to align their interests with those of donors rather than with those of people in need. The policy prescription that follows from this perspective is withdrawal of aid. This action would force aid-dependent countries to become accountable to their citizens. No longer would government be able to attribute the plight of their citizens to foreign actors.

An intermediate position in this debate is that aid targeted towards projects that benefit people living in poverty can be effective when there is sound governance in recipient countries.

Women and girls

It is hard to imagine a society truly prospering when half of its population is constrained from full participation in its economic and social affairs. In many developing countries, this is the situation facing women and girls. Girls in school face school-related gender-based violence. This violence includes acts that are likely to cause physical, sexual, or psychological harm. Peers or teachers in school or in transit to or from school may perpetrate it. In essence, it stems from hostility towards girls who dare deviate from traditional gender roles of society. According to the World Bank, the share of ever-partnered women who have experience physical or sexual violence or both by an intimate partner is 43 per cent in South Asia, 40 per cent in sub-Saharan Africa, 33 per cent in Latin America and the Caribbean, and 30 per cent in East Asia and the Pacific. (Comparable figures for North America, Europe and Central Asia, and Australia and New Zealand are 21 per cent, 29 per cent, and 28 per cent, respectively.)

The impact of this violence is to discourage educational attainment. Less-educated girls grow up to be less-educated women who are disempowered and less productive. Traditional and culturally determined gender roles are more likely to trap less productive women. These roles include childbearing/rearing and provision of basic household services. They are less likely to own land and more likely to be excluded from the political processes of society. Women with a primary school education or less are three times more likely to experience deprivations in control over resources, child marriage (18 years old or younger), and to condone wife beating than their counterparts with a secondary education and higher.

There is evidence, however, that even in the face of existing social norms, well-targeted interventions that empower girls and young women can improve their well-being. One such intervention is the introduction of community-based development clubs that teach girls and young women vocational and life skills. The relevant vocational skills include income-generating activities such as tailoring, computing, and trading. The relevant life skills include preservation of sexual and reproductive health, family planning, and awareness of sexually transmitted diseases. In a randomized control trial (RCT) in Uganda conducted by Oriana Bandiera and her collaborators, girls living in villages that received a community-based development club had higher labour force participation rates, lower teen pregnancy rates, higher consumption levels, and more senior marriage age aspirations than girls in control group villages. We discuss RCTs further in the next section.

Even in developed countries, women face unique challenges based on gender. In the United States, approximately 60 per cent of the adults (aged 18 and over) living in poverty are women. The poverty rate for women is at least 30 per cent higher than it is for men. Important sources of this disparity in rates of poverty incidence are differential pay, occupational choice, and family structure. If women do not receive equal pay for equal work, then discrimination will depress their earnings and make them more susceptible to bouts of poverty. Social norms can serve as barriers to job choice even in developed economies. Society can socialize girls into thinking that certain jobs are more appropriate for them. Frequently, the jobs that society channels girls and women towards are lower paying. Households headed by women experience poverty at a high rate. This is because on average women who head such households have lower educational attainment, fewer resources to spread across all household members, greater odds of a disruption in labour force participation, and limited support for childcare.

Evidence from the UK indicates how educational systems and labour markets confront girls and women with difficult choices and outcomes. In Figure 8, we see the continuation of a trend that emerged in the United Kingdom in the late 1990s; women enter university at a higher rate than men. Other things held equal, you would think that higher rates of university entry would translate into lower risk of economic jeopardy for women relative to men. Yet, women are more likely to live in poverty long term in the UK. Figure 9 shows the persistent poverty rate in the UK. This rate excludes households who live in poverty for short stints

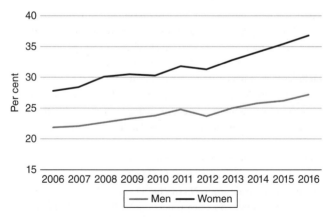

8. **University entry rates by gender in the United Kingdom.**

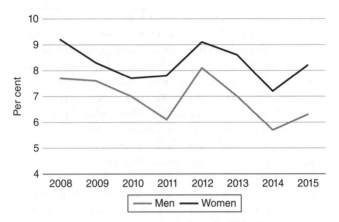

9. **Persistent poverty rate by gender in the United Kingdom.**

due to, say, temporary illness or unemployment of a main earner. Over time, women experience worse long-term economic outcomes at a higher rate than men do. According to human capital theory, however, their relatively high rate of schooling acquisition should make them relatively more productive in the labour market.

These findings suggest that it is essential that we examine the role of social norms more carefully. A pervasive and persistent social norm that affects women worldwide is the disproportionate share of unpaid care work they perform. Unpaid care work includes tasks such as caring for children and elderly adults, cooking, cleaning, and running errands. In the developing country context, we add fetching water and collecting firewood to the list. Unpaid care work limits market-based activities of women.

OECD researchers use time-use surveys to document allocation of unpaid care work by gender worldwide. Figures 10, 11, and 12 summarize their findings. No matter where we look, the finding is the same: women do a disproportionate share of unpaid care work. This finding is robust to variations in culture, legal and

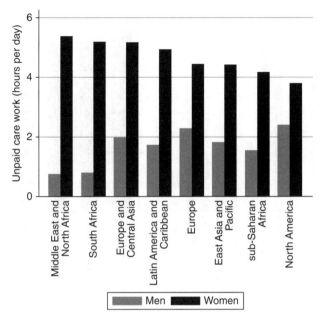

10. **Time spent on unpaid care work by gender and region.**

political systems, income, and geography. In Figure 12, we see
that the only countries that are close to gender equity in unpaid
work are the Nordic countries Denmark, Finland, Norway, and
Sweden. These countries have extensive social safety nets and
parental leave laws that provide incentives for fathers to take
time off from work in order to care for children.

The OECD tracks five categories of social and institutional
arrangements that preserve traditional gender roles: discriminatory
family codes, restricted physical integrity, son bias, restricted
resources and assets, and restricted civil liberties. An alternative to
this state of affairs for women and girls is agency and voice. Agency
is the ability to decide and act on one's own behalf. Voice is
freedom to express one's views and for others to hear you. Together

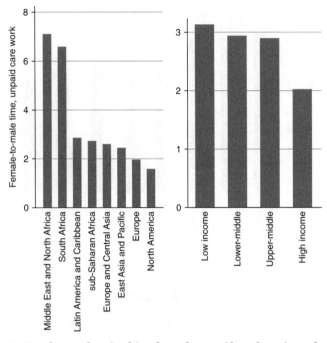

11. Female-to-male ratio of time devoted to unpaid care by region and country income.

they represent empowerment for women. With empowerment comes the possibility of greater educational attainment, more control over fertility, increased chances of property ownership, increased social status, and political influence. Key mechanisms for unleashing the productive talents of women are reforms that change social norms and the introduction and enforcement of laws that prohibit discrimination against women.

Evaluation

What policies or programmes reduce poverty? How do we know what works and what does not work? These questions concern

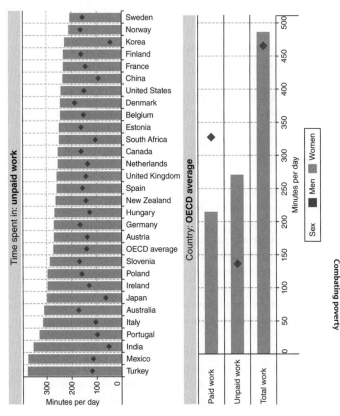

12. **Time spent in paid and unpaid care work by gender.**

policymakers, donors, and NGOs who must decide how to allocate limited resources across competing demands. To answer these questions, we must be able to determine cause and effect.

In the natural sciences, cause and effect are determined by means of experimentation using an RCT. That is, scientists randomly assign study participants into treatment and control groups. Because of random assignment, these groups are identical statistically. The treatment group receives the treatment that scientists are testing for effectiveness. The control group receives a placebo. Scientists then observe both groups over time. Scientists monitor the treatment group to see whether the treatment has an impact on an outcome of concern. The control group provides the counterfactual. That is, it indicates what would likely happen in the treatment group with respect to the outcome of concern had the treatment group not received the treatment. By comparing the average outcome in the treatment and control groups, scientists determine whether the treatment had a statistically significant impact on the outcome variable of concern.

Researchers also use RCTs to determine cause and effect in the social sciences. Their deployment has been especially prominent in evaluating policies and programmes aimed at reducing poverty in developing countries. Examples of programmes that can be evaluated in this way include productive asset transfers (of livestock, for example), cash transfers, technical skill training, and health education. We want to know whether providing people living in poverty with access to these programmes helps them to transition out of extreme poverty, or at least improve their well-being.

Evaluation of such programmes by researchers usually requires local partners who assist with implementation of the RCT. These local partners may be NGOs who have been working on-site (within villages, for example) and are familiar with the local population.

The unit of observation may be households or the village itself. Selection of the unit of observation determines the entity that will populate treatment and control groups. For example, if the household is the unit of observation, then households constitute the treatment and control groups. For exposition purposes, let us consider a situation where households are the unit of observation.

Given this choice, researchers randomly assign each household to either a treatment or control group. Typically, a lottery performs the randomization. After random assignment, researchers examine treatment and control groups to see if the randomization was successful. They do this by checking whether the two groups are the same on average along various dimensions such as initial consumption, income, and health.

Once researchers establish that the randomization was successful, it is possible to begin implementation of a programme. The next step in an RCT is to allow the programme to be in effect for some period. In the case of a cash transfer programme, for example, researchers make monthly cash payments to treatment households for a year.

Researchers determine the effectiveness of a programme by whether it has a lasting impact. To assess this, they return to the village after the end of the programme, say one year later. Of course, what they want to know is whether the treatment group is measurably better off relative to the control group. If the answer to this question is yes, then there is increased confidence that the programme reduces poverty or at least improves well-being. Researchers use the RCT method of programme evaluation in many countries throughout the developing world.

Because of their large scale, however, not all anti-poverty programmes and policies lend themselves to evaluation via RCTs. When this is the case, we have to appeal to alternative methods of evaluation. If a programme is already in existence, there may be circumstances where researchers can use changes in the programme that government implements unevenly in a temporal or spatial sense to evaluate the effectiveness of the programme.

An example from the United States is expansions in Medicaid, the means-tested federal government health insurance programme. Medicaid mainly covers low-income women, children, elderly adults, and the disabled. Individual states administer and implement it. The states also have some discretion over eligibility.

Therefore, one state may not match policy changes in another state. For example, one state could decide to expand eligibility while a neighbouring state could maintain its status quo with respect to Medicaid eligibility. If the neighbouring state is otherwise quite similar to the eligibility-expanding state, then it may be possible to learn something about the impact of expanding Medicaid coverage on health outcomes. If we believed that before the Medicaid expansion, the average health status of citizens in the two states evolved over time in the same way, then we could compare the change in average health status of citizens in the eligibility-expanding state with the change in average health status of citizens in the neighbouring status quo state. In both states, the change is simply the difference between average health status before and average health status after the date of eligibility expansion. If the difference in changes between states is significant and, say, positive, then we would conclude that the eligibility expansion improved the health status and thereby the well-being of low-income citizens in the eligibility-expanding state.

This is an example of a natural (or quasi-natural) experiment. Conceptually, researchers consider citizens in the eligibility-expanding state as the treatment group. The treatment is receipt of insurance by the previously uninsured, the expansion of health insurance via Medicaid. Citizens of the neighbouring status quo state are the control group. As always, the control group provides the counterfactual; an estimate of the outcome in the treatment group if it had not been treated. Comparison of the changes in both states across the date of the policy change in the eligibility-expanding state allows us to determine what a significant change in the outcome variable is. The change in the outcome variable in the neighbouring state is the benchmark for comparison. If the change in the outcome variable in the eligibility-expanding state were not much different from the benchmark, then we would conclude that the policy did not have a significant effect. There are variants of the natural experimentation approach to programme evaluation. With respect to expansion of health insurance to low-income people in the United States, for example, evidence compiled from natural experiments suggests that such expansions have beneficial effects, including increased healthcare utilization, improved infant health, and a reduction in preventable hospitalizations.

Another approach to policy and programme evaluation compares pre-transfer and post-transfer statuses of a household to a given poverty threshold. Post-transfer, it asks whether a household is still deemed to be living in poverty or not. If the post-transfer income level, for example, is greater than the poverty income threshold, then researchers give credit for lifting the household out of poverty to the programme that granted the transfer. This approach to programme evaluation allows us to consider the impact of a given programme on the aggregate poverty rate. Given information about benefit receipt on a large sample of households, we can conceptually reposition them relative to the poverty line by recalculating their income in the absence of the transfer. If researchers analyse the programmes that make up a society's social safety net in this way, then it is possible to estimate the total effectiveness of the social safety net at reducing poverty.

Finally, there is evaluation based on history. Sometimes historians can only assess appropriately what works with the benefit of hindsight. In retrospect, economic historians such as Angus Maddison highlight certain features that were present in England and Western Europe that catalysed industrialization, growth, and eventually mass poverty reduction. Those features include establishment of universities that leveraged the development of printing for purposes of disseminating technical knowledge, nondiscretionary recognition of property rights and contract enforcement, adoption of strict social norms around the structure of the family imposed by the Church, and the rise of trading centres that enhanced the rewards from entrepreneurial activity.

The historical approach to evaluation has much to recommend it because what may have seemed effective at the time does not always last. Ultimately, advances in knowledge and technological change are engines of growth. Robert Fogel documents, however, that even the Industrial Revolution in England and Europe took more than a century to bring sustained increases in physical stature (height and weight) and improved dietary quality to labourers and farmers. Here was well-being lagging behind growth and development. Further, Angus Deaton reminds us that policy follies (the Great Leap Forward in China) or disease (the HIV/AIDS pandemic in sub-Saharan Africa) can undo growth and poverty reduction.

Policy design and evaluation arise from the need to know what reduces poverty. The knowledge gained from rigorous policy analysis stimulates campaigns to eradicate extreme poverty.

Chapter 8
Whither poverty?

Making the case

Is it becoming easier to envision a world without extreme poverty? That goal is still some way off, but there have been moments where it seems that because we focused our attention on poverty eradication, some actual poverty reduction occurred. When were those moments? How did poverty eradication make its way on to the public agenda? What did we achieve during those moments? What are the prospects for designing and executing the final poverty eradication initiative in the future? Post-1960, there have been multiple attempts to place poverty reduction on the public agenda. Three of those attempts are the war on poverty, the Millennium Development Goals, and the Sustainable Development Goals.

Mass anti-poverty initiatives past

On 8 January 1964, President Lyndon B. Johnson declared 'unconditional war on poverty in America' in his State of the Union Address. Central command in the War on Poverty was the Office of Economic Opportunity (OEO). The OEO was composed of two divisions: The Community Action Program (CAP) and Research, Programming, Planning, and Evaluation (RPP&E). The historian Alice O'Connor documents the role of each division.

The CAP was concerned with ensuring that people living in poverty had a say in the implementation of policies and programmes that affected them. It fostered community organizing and engagement through the establishment of NGOs operating at the local level. The RPP&E focused on systematic analyses of poverty. It was concerned with using data gathered from nationally representative surveys conducted at the individual or household level to understand those living in poverty. It was also one of the first government agencies to promote RCTs as the standard for evaluation of whether an anti-poverty programme was effective. While the OEO has long since disappeared, it is noteworthy that anti-poverty practitioners still deploy principles that originated there. These principles include use of experiments to determine programme effectiveness, use of NGOs as on-the-ground implementation partners, and encouragement of participation by members of the community being served.

There has been much debate about whether we won or lost the war on poverty. There can be little doubt, however, that President Johnson's 1964 State of the Union address is an exemplary call to action against poverty in a democratic society. The objective of finding a cure to poverty and empowerment through opportunity has endured as a pillar of the anti-poverty agenda not only in the United States but worldwide. Johnson's declaration provided a template for action against poverty on a global scale.

On 8 September 2000, the General Assembly of the United Nations adopted Resolution 55/2: United Nations Millennium Declaration. Contained in that resolution were eight Millennium Development Goals (MDGs) with a deadline of 2015 for achievement. Associated with these goals were eighteen targets that participants used to assess whether a given goal was satisfied. For example, associated with Goal 1 (eradicate extreme hunger and poverty) was the target: 'halve, by the year 2015, the proportion of the world's people whose income is less than one dollar a day and the proportion of people who suffer from hunger and, by the same date, to halve the proportion of people who are unable to reach or to afford safe drinking water'. Associated with Goal 3 (promote gender equality and empower women) was the target: 'ensure that, by the same date, children everywhere, boys and girls alike, will be able to complete a full course of primary schooling and that girls and boys will have equal access to all levels of education'.

To achieve these goals, participating countries would have to adopt policies and programmes that benefited their most disadvantaged citizens. Donor organizations and donor countries stood ready to provide aid to developing countries lacking the fiscal capacity to finance necessary programmes and initiatives. In this way, the MDGs rallied the donor community worldwide by providing it with a clear set of objectives and a deadline for achieving them.

Did participants achieve the MDGs? The United Nations asserts that participants made significant progress towards each goal. It cites examples from the developing world between 1990 and 2015. The proportion of people living in extreme poverty fell from about 50 per cent to around 14 per cent. The proportion of undernourished people fell from 23.3 per cent to about 13 per cent. Several countries eliminated disparity between boys and girls in enrolment in primary, secondary, and tertiary education. The number of deaths of children under five years old declined from about thirteen million to about six million. In South Asia and in sub-Saharan Africa, the maternal mortality rate (deaths per 100,000 live births) fell by more than 45 per cent. Insecticide-treated mosquito nets contributed to the prevention of millions of deaths due to malaria in sub-Saharan Africa. The proportion of the urban population living in slums fell from about 39 per cent to about 30 per cent between 2000 and 2014.

Critics ask, however, were these achievements because of the MDGs? First, as we saw in Chapter 7, establishing cause and effect is complicated in the absence of a counterfactual. We do not have one here. Therefore, it is difficult to isolate the effect of the goals from other factors. We do not know what would have happened if the United Nations had not enacted the MDGs. Second, the timing is awkward. The MDGs came into effect in 2000. By then, China had been growing rapidly for more than a decade. As a result, economic growth was already reducing extreme poverty rapidly in the most populous country in the world. Thus, it is difficult to attribute most of the worldwide reduction in extreme poverty (Goal 1) since 1990 to the MDGs. Third, school enrolment numbers are the basis for achievement of Goal 2 (achieve universal primary education). As we know from the examples in Chapter 4, however, in the developing country context and in the developed country context, there can be a distinction between school enrolment and actual learning. MDG critics would argue that Goal 2 misses the mark on what matters for individual well-being.

The controversy over the accomplishments of the MDGs notwithstanding, as 2015 ended, it was clear that gaps remained: over 800 million people worldwide still lived in extreme poverty; income inequality within and across nations was severe; levels of greenhouse gases emissions increased; women faced discrimination in the labour market; and armed conflict displaced millions of people. These gaps between the aspirations of the MDGs and observed outcomes provided impetus for another round of goal setting by the international community that might finish the job.

Mass anti-poverty initiatives present

On 25 September 2015, the General Assembly of the United Nations adopted Resolution 70/1; Transforming Our World: The 2030 Agenda for Sustainable Development. Contained in that resolution are seventeen Sustainable Development Goals (SDGs). For the United Nations, these goals are interdependent. A number of subsidiary targets are associated with each goal. Cumulatively, there are over one hundred such targets. The targets serve as benchmarks that observers can use to assess whether the world has achieved the associated goal. For example, associated with Goal 1 (end poverty in all its forms everywhere) is the target: 'By 2030, eradicate extreme poverty for all people everywhere, currently measured as people living on less than $1.25 a day.' Since the United Nations passed this resolution, the World Bank revised the international poverty line for extreme poverty upward to $1.90 a day. Nevertheless, the point of emphasis is the same. Associated with Goal 10 (reduce inequality within and among countries) is the target: 'By 2030, progressively achieve and sustain income growth of the bottom 40% of the population at a rate higher than the national average.' Goal 10 makes salient the concern with how economies distribute the benefits of growth across the population. For the World Bank, this target is emblematic of 'shared prosperity'. Along with poverty reduction, stimulating income growth in the bottom 40 per cent of the income distribution will guide the World Bank's work in support of the SDGs.

Critics ask, is it possible to focus on seventeen goals with more than one hundred targets? First, the United Nations does not prioritize the SDGs. Developing countries, however, have limited fiscal capacity in terms of raising tax revenue or borrowing. In addition, donor aid is limited. At the margin, each goal competes for the next available dollar. Without any prioritization, on what basis do we decide how to spend that next dollar?

Second, looking ahead, extreme poverty is likely to be concentrated in fragile states. How do traditional approaches to development map into such volatile circumstances, if at all? The government is either too weak or too non-representative. The situation is too unstable for non-government actors (NGOs, faith-based organizations, and private charities) to make long-term commitments. Therefore, it is difficult to find reliable partners on the ground.

The OECD defines state fragility along a continuum where a country faces challenges in one or more of five dimensions: violence, justice, institutions, economic foundations, and resilience. At various points in this book, we have highlighted each of these dimensions. Thus, we are succinct here. Violence is the use of extreme physical force. It is problematic when the state has not monopolized its use. Justice is the rule of law and equal access to and protection under the law. Rules that insure inclusive and effective political and economic processes are good institutions. Broad access to quality education and markets are foundational for economic growth and equitably shared prosperity. Because markets fail sometimes and because countries are vulnerable to unpredictable internal and external shocks, social safety nets make countries more resilient. A state becomes more fragile when it moves in the wrong direction along any one of these dimensions.

The not-for-profit research organization Fund for Peace publishes a Fragile State Index annually. This index locates countries on the fragility continuum. Table 13 reports the five most, five median, and five least fragile countries in 2007 and 2017. The composition of each tier changes over time in response to events. Negative shocks such as natural disasters, warfare, or disease can cause countries to become more fragile. Positive shocks such as good governance can cause countries to become more stable and less fragile. These outcomes are consistent with fluidity across the fragility continuum. The consistent membership of the least fragile tier is notable, however. According to the World Bank, all of the countries in the least fragile tier are high-income countries. Countries in the 2017 least fragile group also have robust social safety nets. No country stayed at the median of the distribution over time. The 2017 group in that tier are either lower-middle-income (El Salvador, Tunisia, and Ukraine) or upper-middle-income (Mexico and Gabon) countries. In 2017, the most fragile countries have conflict in common. They are also either low-income

134

Table 13 Fragile states

	2007	2017
Most fragile	Sudan	South Sudan*
	Iraq	Somalia
	Somalia	Central African Republic
	Zimbabwe	Yemen
	Chad	Syria
Median fragile	Peru	Mexico
	Gambia	Tunisia
	Thailand	Ukraine
	Morocco	Gabon
	Algeria	El Salvador
Least fragile	Switzerland	Sweden
	Ireland	Denmark
	Sweden	Switzerland
	Finland	Norway
	Norway	Finland

N.B. * South Sudan gained independence from Sudan in 2011.

Fragile states rankings based on Fragile States Index, from Fund for Peace <http://fundforpeace.org/fsi/>.

(South Sudan, Somalia, Central African Republic) or lower-middle-income countries (Yemen, Syria).

Low-income conflict-ridden (or post-conflict) countries emit populations yearning for a better future. Large-scale migrations risk overwhelming destination countries. They may strain social safety nets, accentuate political tensions, and invigorate latent ethnic animosities in countries that receive displaced people. In this way, fragility cascades geographically and temporally. Stinting this cascade requires policies and diplomacy that create lasting peace. In the absence of peace, sustained poverty eradication is elusive.

In the year 2030, there will still be people living in poverty. Most likely, they will be concentrated in fragile states. There will be a need for another poverty eradication initiative. The targets of that initiative will be areas or peoples where it may be far harder to make progress with respect to better schooling and health, gender equality, inclusivity, democracy, rule of law, peace, environmental sustainability, and all of the other concomitants of shared prosperity.

Conclusion

In Chapter 1, we considered why poverty matters. We cited examples where poverty may have been a source of social unrest and political upheaval. We also highlighted moral or ethical reasons why society might care about poverty. Poverty deprives people of the opportunity to live their lives to its fullest. The goal of action against poverty is creation of a world where every individual's opportunity to thrive (not just survive) can be independent of the circumstances of her birth, if she chooses. If we focus solely on individual outcomes, however, we risk forgetting a collective reason why poverty matters. In 1937, when much of the world was living in poverty, President Franklin D. Roosevelt articulated a meaningful measure of human progress in his Second Inaugural Address: 'The test of our progress is not whether we add more to the abundance of those who have much; it is whether we provide enough for those who have too little.' Poverty matters because it is an obstacle to our progress, properly defined.

Further reading

I draw upon many published studies, working papers, books, databases, newspaper and magazine articles, websites, government documents, and documents published by international organizations. Space restrictions necessitate that I list only selected further reading here.

Chapter 1: Introduction

Autor, David, David Dorn, and Gordon Hanson (2016) 'The China Shock: Learning from Labor Market Adjustment to Large Changes in Trade', *Annual Review of Economics* Vol. 8, pp. 205–40.

Rawls, John (1971) *A Theory of Justice*, Harvard University Press, Cambridge, MA.

Rothstein, Richard (2017) *The Color of Law: A Forgotten History of How Our Government Segregated America*, Liveright Publishing Corporation, New York.

Chapter 2: History

Chernow, Ron (2004) *Alexander Hamilton*, The Penguin Press, New York.

Maddison, Angus (2013) *The Maddison-Project*, <http://www.ggdc.net/maddison/maddison-project/home.htm>, 2013 version.

Malthus, Thomas Robert (1798) *An Essay on the Principle of Population: As It Affects the Future Improvement of Society*, J. Johnson, London.

Marx, Karl (1867, originally published in German) *Capital: A Critique of Political Economy*, Progress Publishers, 1954–9, Moscow.

Ricardo, David (1817) *On the Principles of Political Economy and Taxation*, John Murray, London.

Smith, Adam (1776) *An Inquiry into the Nature and Causes of the Wealth of Nations*, edited by Edwin Cannan, with a Preface by George J. Stigler, 1977, University of Chicago Press, Chicago.

Williamson, Jeffrey G. (2011) *Trade and Poverty: When the Third World Fell Behind*, MIT Press, Cambridge, MA.

Chapter 3: Measurement

Citro, Constance F. and Robert T. Michael, eds (1995) *Measuring Poverty: A New Approach*, National Academy Press, Washington, DC.

Foster, James, Joel Greer, and Erik Thorbecke (1984) 'A Class of Decomposable Poverty Measures', *Econometrica* Vol. 52, No. 3, pp. 761–6.

Nussbaum, Martha (1999) 'Women and Equality: The Capabilities Approach', *International Labour Review*, Vol. 138, No. 3, pp. 227–45.

Sen, Amartya (1999) 'The Possibility of Social Choice', *American Economic Review*, Vol. 89, No. 3, pp. 349–78.

Chapter 4: Living: here and there

Banerjee, Abhijit V. and Esther Duflo (2007) 'The Economic Lives of the Poor', *Journal of Economic Perspectives*, Vol. 21, No. 1, pp. 141–67.

Barrow, Lisa and Diane Whitmore Schanzenbach (2012) 'Education and the Poor', in *The Oxford Handbook of the Economics of Poverty*, edited by Philip N. Jefferson, pp. 316–43, Oxford University Press, New York.

Chen, Alice, Emily Oster, and Heidi Williams (2016) 'Why is Infant Mortality Higher in the United States than in Europe?', *American Economic Journal: Economic Policy*, Vol. 8, No. 2, pp. 89–124.

Chapter 5: Labour markets

Arrow, Kenneth J. (1972) 'Models of Job Discrimination', in *Racial Discrimination in Economic Life*, edited by Anthony H. Pascal, DC pp. 83–103, Heath, Lexington, MA.

Becker, Gary S. (1957) *The Economics of Discrimination*, University of Chicago Press, Chicago.

Bhorat, Haroon, Ravi Kanbur, and Benjamin Stanwix (2015) 'Minimum Wages in Sub-Saharan Africa: A Primer', *IZA Discussion Paper*, No. 9204.

Blau, Francine D. and Lawrence M. Kahn (2017) 'The Gender Wage Gap: Extent, Trends, and Explanations', *Journal of Economic Literature*, Vol. 55, No. 3, pp. 789–865.

Blinder, Alan (1973) 'Wage Discrimination: Reduced Form and Structural Estimates', *Journal of Human Resources*, Vol. 8, No. 4, pp. 436–55.

Dube, Arindrajit (2017) 'Minimum Wages and the Distribution of Family Incomes', *IZA Discussion Paper*, No. 10572.

Duncan, Brian and Stephen Trejo (2012) 'Low-Skilled Immigrants and the US Labor Market', in *The Oxford Handbook of the Economics of Poverty*, edited by Philip N. Jefferson, pp. 203–48, Oxford University Press, New York.

Oaxaca, Ronald (1973) 'Male–Female Wage Differences in Urban Labor Markets', *International Economic Review*, Vol. 14, No. 3, pp. 693–709.

Pager, Devah, Bruce Western, and Bart Bonikowski (2009) 'Discrimination in a Low-Wage Labor Market: A Field Experiment', *American Sociological Review*, Vol. 74, No. 5, pp. 777–99.

Peet, Evan D., Günther Fink, and Wafaie Fawzi (2015) 'Returns to Education in Developing Countries: Evidence from the Living Standards and Measurement Study Surveys', *Economics of Education Review*, Vol. 49, pp. 69–90.

Phelps, Edmund S. (1972) 'The Statistical Theory of Racism and Sexism', *American Economic Review*, Vol. 62, No. 4, pp. 659–61.

Chapter 6: Distribution and mobility

Chetty, Raj and Nathaniel Hendren (2017) 'The Effects of Neighborhoods on Intergenerational Mobility I: Childhood Exposure Effects', *National Bureau of Economic Research Working Paper*, No. 23001.

Corak, Miles (2016) 'Inequality from Generation to Generation: The United States in Comparison', *IZA Discussion Paper*, No. 9929.

Gini, Corrado (1912) *Variabilità e Mutabilità*, C. Cuppini, Bologna.

Pew Research Center (2014) *Emerging and Developing Economies Much More Optimistic than Rich Countries About the Future*, Washington, DC.

Solon, Gary (2004) 'A Model of Intergenerational Mobility Variation Over Time and Place', in *Generational Income Mobility in North America and Europe*, edited by Miles Corak, pp. 38–47, Cambridge University Press, Cambridge.

Steele, Claude M. and Joshua A. Aronson (1995) 'Stereotype Threat and the Intellectual Test Performance of African Americans', *Journal of Personality and Social Psychology*, Vol. 69, No. 5, pp. 797–811.

Stevens, Ann Huff (2012) 'Poverty Transitions', in *The Oxford Handbook of the Economics of Poverty*, edited by Philip N. Jefferson, pp. 494–518, Oxford University Press, New York.

Wilson, William Julius (1987) *The Truly Disadvantaged: The Inner City, the Underclass and Public Policy*, University of Chicago Press, Chicago.

Chapter 7: Combating poverty

Acemoglu, Daron and James Robinson (2012) *Why Nations Fail: The Origins of Power, Prosperity, and Poverty*, Crown Business, New York.

Bandiera, Oriana, Niklas Buehren, Robin Burgess, Markus Goldstein, Selim Gulesci, Imran Rasul, and Munshi Sulaimany (2017) 'Women's Empowerment in Action: Evidence from a Randomized Control Trial in Africa', working paper.

Bhattacharya, Amar, Mattia Romani, and Nicholas Stern (2012) 'Infrastructure for Development: Meeting the Challenge', policy paper, Centre for Climate Change Economics and Policy Grantham Research Institute on Climate Change and the Environment, London.

Bono (2009) 'It's 2009: Do You Know Where Your Soul Is?', *New York Times*, 8 April 2009.

Deaton, Angus (2013) *The Great Escape: Health, Wealth, and the Origins of Inequality*, Princeton University Press, Princeton, NJ.

Easterly, William (2006) *The White Man's Burden. Why the West's Efforts to Aid the Rest Have Done So Much Ill and So Little Good*, Penguin Press, New York.

Fogel, Robert W. (2004) *The Escape from Hunger and Premature Death, 1700–2100: Europe, America, and the Third World*, Cambridge University Press, Cambridge.

Maddison, Angus (2007) *Contours of the World Economy, 1–2030 AD: Essays in Macro-Economic History*, Oxford University Press, New York.

Moyo, Dambisa (2009) *Dead Aid: Why Aid is Not Working and How There is a Better Way for Africa*, Farrar, Straus and Giroux, New York.

Pring, Coralie (2015) *People and Corruption: African Survey 2015*, Transparency International, Berlin.

Ravallion, Martin (2011) 'A Comparative Perspective on Poverty Reduction in Brazil, China, and India', *World Bank Research Observer*, Vol. 26, No. 1, pp. 71–104.

Sachs, Jeffrey (2014) 'The Case for Aid', *Foreign Policy*, online, 14 January 2014.

World Bank (2015) *The State of Social Safety Nets 2015*, World Bank, Washington, DC.

Chapter 8: Whither poverty?

Fund for Peace (2017) *2017 Fragile States Index*, Washington, DC.

O'Connor, Alice (2001) *Poverty Knowledge: Social Science, Social Policy and the Poor in Twentieth-Century U.S. History*, Princeton University Press, Princeton, NJ.

OECD (2015) *States of Fragility 2015: Meeting Post-2015 Ambitions*, OECD Publishing, Paris.

Index

GLOBALIZATION
A Very Short Introduction
Manfred Steger

'Globalization' has become one of the defining buzzwords
of our time - a term that describes a variety of accelerating
economic, political, cultural, ideological, and environmental
processes that are rapidly altering our experience of the world.
It is by its nature a dynamic topic - and this *Very Short
Introduction* has been fully updated for 2009, to include
developments in global politics, the impact of terrorism, and
environmental issues. Presenting globalization in accessible
language as a multifaceted process encompassing global,
regional, and local aspects of social life, Manfred B. Steger
looks at its causes and effects, examines whether it is a new
phenomenon, and explores the question of whether,
ultimately, globalization is a good or a bad thing.

www.oup.com/vsi

ANTISEMITISM
A Very Short Introduction
Steven Beller

Antisemitism - a prejudice against or hatred of Jews - has been a chillingly persistent presence throughout the last millennium, culminating in the dark apogee of the Holocaust. This *Very Short Introduction* examines and untangles the various strands of antisemitism seen throughout history, from medieval religious conflict to 'new' antisemitism in the 21st century. Steven Beller reveals how the phenomenon grew as a political and ideological movement in the 19th century, how it reached it its dark apogee in the worst genocide in modern history - the Holocaust - and how antisemitism still persists around the world today.

www.oup.com/vsi

COMMUNISM
A Very Short Introduction
Leslie Holmes

The collapse of communism was one of the most defining moments of the twentieth century. At its peak, more than a third of the world's population had lived under communist power. What is communism? Where did the idea come from and what attracted people to it? What is the future for communism? This Very Short Introduction considers these questions and more in the search to explore and understand communism. Explaining the theory behind its ideology, and examining the history and mindset behind its political, economic and social structures, Leslie Holmes examines the highs and lows of communist power and its future in today's world.

Very readable and with its wealth of detail a most valuable reference book.

Gwyn Griffiths, Morning Star

www.oup.com/vsi

ECONOMICS
A Very Short Introduction
Partha Dasgupta

Economics has the capacity to offer us deep insights into some of the most formidable problems of life, and offer solutions to them too. Combining a global approach with examples from everyday life, Partha Dasgupta describes the lives of two children who live very different lives in different parts of the world: in the Mid-West USA and in Ethiopia. He compares the obstacles facing them, and the processes that shape their lives, their families, and their futures. He shows how economics uncovers these processes, finds explanations for them, and how it forms policies and solutions.

'An excellent introduction . . . presents mathematical and statistical findings in straightforward prose.'

Financial Times

GEOPOLITICS
A Very Short Introduction
Klaus Dodds

In certain places such as Iraq or Lebanon, moving a few feet either side of a territorial boundary can be a matter of life or death, dramatically highlighting the connections between place and politics. For a country's location and size as well as its sovereignty and resources all affect how the people that live there understand and interact with the wider world. Using wide-ranging examples, from historical maps to James Bond films and the rhetoric of political leaders like Churchill and George W. Bush, this Very Short Introduction shows why, for a full understanding of contemporary global politics, it is not just smart - it is essential - to be geopolitical.

'Engrossing study of a complex topic.'

Mick Herron, Geographical.